Tea and Sympathy

A DRAMA IN THREE ACTS

by Robert ~~Woodruff~~ *Anderson* 1917-

SAMUEL FRENCH, INC.
25 WEST 45TH STREET   NEW YORK 10036
7623 SUNSET BOULEVARD   HOLLYWOOD 90046
LONDON   *TORONTO*

3.00

This is for
PHYLLIS
whose spirit is everywhere
in this play and in my life.

TEA AND SYMPATHY

STORY OF THE PLAY
(9 males; 2 females)

Tea and Sympathy is the story of a lonely and mis-
understood youth who, because he has artistic sensibilities
and has played women's parts in amateur theatricals, is
wrongly suspected of homosexual tendencies. Although
the master in whose house he rooms is one of his chief
persecutors, the wife of the teacher is kind and under-
standing, as well as beautiful. The play is pretty specific
about the physical aspects of the resulting relationship,
but it handles it with taste, delicacy and considerable
emotional skill.

Tea and Sympathy was presented at the Barrymore Theatre in New York on September 30, 1953, by The Playwrights Company in association with Mary K. Frank. Scenery and lighting by Jo Mielziner, costumes by Anna Hill Johnstone. It was directed by Elia Kazan, with the following cast:

LAURA REYNOLDS	*Deborah Kerr*
LILLY SEARS	*Florida Friebus*
TOM LEE	*John Kerr*
DAVID HARRIS	*Richard Midgley*
RALPH	*Alan Sues*
AL	*Dick York*
STEVE	*Arthur Steuer*
BILL REYNOLDS	*Leif Erickson*
PHIL	*Richard Franchot*
HERBERT LEE	*John McGovern*
PAUL	*Yale Wexler*

The action of the play takes place in late Spring in the dormitory of a boys' school in New England.

Tea and Sympathy

ACT ONE

SCENE: *The scene is a small old Colonial house which is now being used as a dormitory in a boys' school in New England.*

On the ground floor at stage Right we see the housemaster's study. To stage Left of this is a hall and stairway which leads up to the boys' rooms. At a half level on stage Left is one of the boys' rooms.

The housemaster's study is a warm and friendly room, rather on the dark side, but when the lamps are lighted there are cheerful pools of light. There is a fireplace in the back wall, book cases, and upstage Right double doors leading to another part of the house. Since there is no common room for the eight boys in this house, there is considerable leniency in letting the boys use the study whenever the door is left ajar.

The boy's bedroom is small, containing a bed, a chair and a bureau. It was meant to be Spartan, but the present occupant has given it a few touches to make it a little more homelike—an India print on the bed, India print curtains for the dormer window. There is a phonograph in the room, on the ledge of the window. The door to the room is presumed to lead to the sitting room which the roommates share. There is a door from the sitting room which leads to the stair landing. Thus to get to the bedroom from the stairs, a person must go through the sitting room. (See ground plan back of book.)

*As the Curtain rises, it is late afternoon of a day early in
    June. No lamps have been lighted yet—so the study
    is in a sort of twilight.*

(Upstairs in his room, TOM LEE *is sitting on his bed
    playing the guitar and singing softly and casually
    the plaintive song, "The Joys of Love."* TOM *is going
    on 18. He is young and a little gangling, but intense.
    He is wearing faded khaki trousers, a white shirt
    open at the neck, and white tennis sneakers.)*

(Seated in the study listening to the singing are LAURA
    REYNOLDS *and* LILLY SEARS. LAURA *is a lovely, sensi-
    tive woman in her mid to late twenties. Her essence
    is gentleness. She is compassionate and tender. She
    is wearing a cashmere sweater and a wool skirt. As
    she listens to* TOM'S *singing, she is sewing on what is
    obviously a period costume.)*

*(*LILLY *is in her late thirties, and in contrast to the simple
    effectiveness of Laura's clothes, she is dressed a little
    too flashily for her surroundings. It would be in good
    taste on East 57th Street, but not in a small New
    England town. A smart suit and hat and a fur-piece.
    As she listens to* TOM *singing, she plays with the
    martini glass in her hand.)*

TOM. *(Singing.)*
>   The joys of love
>   Are but a moment long—
>   The pains of love
>   Endure forever—

*(When he has finished, he strums on over the same melody
very casually, and hums to it intermittently.)*

LILLY. *(While* TOM *is singing.)* Tom Lee?

LAURA. *(In Left armchair.)* Yes.

LILLY. Doesn't he have an afternoon class?

LAURA. No. He's the only one in the house that
doesn't.

LILLY. *(When* TOM *has finished the song.)* Do you know what he's thinking of?

LAURA. *(Bites off a thread and looks up.)* What do you mean?

LILLY. What all the boys in this school are thinking about. Not only now in the Spring, but all the time— Sex! *(She wags her head a little wisely, and smiles.)*

LAURA. Lilly, you just like to shock people.

LILLY. Four hundred boys from the ages of thirteen to nineteen. That's the age, Laura. *(Restless, getting up.)* Doesn't it give you the willies sometimes, having all these boys around?

LAURA. Of course not. I never think of it that way.

LILLY. Harry tells me they put saltpetre in their food to quiet them down. But the way they look at you, I can't believe it.

LAURA. At me?

LILLY. At any woman worth looking at. When I first came here ten years ago, I didn't think I could stand it. Now I love it. I love watching them look and suffer.

LAURA. Lilly.

LILLY. This is your first Spring here, Laura. You wait.

LAURA. They're just boys.

LILLY. The authorities say the ages from thirteen to nineteen—

LAURA. Lilly, honestly!

LILLY. You sound as though you were in the grave. How old are you?

LAURA. *(Smiling.)* Over twenty-one.

LILLY. They come here ignorant as all get-out about women, and then spend the next four years exchanging misinformation.—They're so cute, and so damned intense. *(She shudders again.)*

LAURA. Most of them seem very casual to me.

LILLY. That's just an air they put on.—This is the age Romeo should be played. You'd believe him! So intense! These kids would die for love or almost anything else. Harry says all their themes end in death.

LAURA. That's boys.

LILLY. Failure; death! Dishonor; death! Lose their girls; death! It's gruesome.

LAURA. But rather touching too, don't you think?

LILLY. You won't tell your husband the way I was talking?

LAURA. Of course not.

LILLY. Though I don't know why I should care. All the boys talk about me. They have me in and out of bed with every single master in the school—and some married ones, too.

LAURA. *(Kidding her.)* Maybe I'd better listen to them.

LILLY. Oh, never with your husband, of course.

LAURA. Thanks.

LILLY. Even before he met you, Bill never gave me a second glance. He was all the time organizing teams, planning Mountain Club Outings.

LAURA. Bill's good at that sort of thing; he likes it.

LILLY. And you?

(LAURA *looks up at* LILLY *and smiles.)*
Not a very cooperative witness, are you? I know, mind my own business. But watch out he doesn't drag his usual quota of boys to the lodge in Maine this summer.

LAURA. I've got my own plans for him. *(She picks up some vacation folders.)*

LILLY. Oh really? What?

LAURA. "Come to Canada."—I want to get him off on a trip alone.

LILLY. I don't blame you.

LAURA. *(Reflecting.)* Of course I'd really like to go back to Italy. We had a good time there last summer. It was wonderful then. You should have seen Bill.

LILLY. Look, Honey, you married Bill last year on his sabbatical leave, and abroad to boot. Teachers on sabbatical leave abroad are like men in uniform during the war. They never look so good again.

LAURA. Bill looks all right to me.

LILLY. Did Bill ever tell you about the party we gave him before his sabbatical?

LAURA. Yes. I have a souvenir from it. *(She is wearing a rather large Woolworth's diamond ring on a gold chain around her neck. She now pulls it out from her sweater.)*

LILLY. I never thought he'd use that Five and Dime engagement ring we gave him that night. Even though we gave him an awful ribbing, we all expected him to come back a bachelor.

LAURA. You make it sound as though you kidded him into marrying.

LILLY. Oh, no, Honey, it wasn't that.

LAURA. *(With meaning.)* No, it wasn't. (LAURA *laughs at* LILLY.)

LILLY. Well, I've got to go. You know, Bill could have married any number of the right kind of girls around here. But I knew it would take more than the right kind of girl to get Bill to marry. It would take something special. And you're something special.

LAURA. How should I take that?

LILLY. As a compliment. Thanks for the drink. Don't tell Harry I had one when you see him at dinner.

LAURA. We won't be over to the hall. I've laid in a sort of feast for tonight.

LILLY. Celebrating something?

LAURA. No, just an impulse.

LILLY. Well, don't tell Harry anyway.

LAURA. You'd better stop talking the way you've been talking, or I won't have to tell him.

LILLY. Now, look, Honey, don't you start going Puritan on me. You're the only one in this school I can shoot my mouth off to, so don't change, Baby. Don't change.

LAURA. I won't.

LILLY. Some day I'm going to wheedle out of you all the juicy stories you must have from when you were in the theatre.

LAURA. Lilly, you would make the most hardened chorus girl blush.

LILLY. *(Pleased.)* Really?

LAURA. Really.

LILLY. That's the sweetest thing you've said to me in

days— Goodbye. *(She goes out the door to hall, and a moment later we hear the outside DOOR close.)*

LAURA. *(Sits for a moment, listening to* TOM's *rather plaintive whistling. She rises and looks at the Canada vacation literature on the desk, and then, looking at her watch, goes to the door, opens it, and calls up the stairway.)* Tom— Oh, Tom.

TOM. *(The moment* TOM *hears his name, he jumps from the bed, and goes through the sitting room, and appears on the stairs.)* Yes?

LAURA. *(She is very friendly with him—comradely.)* If it won't spoil your supper, come on down for a cup of tea.

   (TOM goes back into his room and brushes his hair, then he comes on down the stairs, and enters the study. He enters this room as though it were something rare and special. This is where LAURA *lives.)*

*(*LAURA *has gone out through the alcove to the other part of the house.)* I've just about finished your costume for the play, and we can have a fitting.

TOM. Sure. That'd be great— Do you want the door open or shut?

LAURA. *(Offstage.)* It doesn't make any difference.

   (TOM shuts the hall door. He is deeply in love with this woman, though he knows nothing can come of it. It is a sort of delayed puppy love. It is very touching and very intense. They are easy with each other, casual, though he is always trying in thinly veiled ways to tell her he loves her.)

*(*LAURA *enters with tea tray and sees him closing the door. She puts tray on table Center.)* Perhaps you'd better leave it ajar, so that if some of the other boys get out of class early, they can come in too.

TOM. *(Is disappointed.)* Oh, sure.

LAURA. *(Goes off for the plate of cookies, but pauses long enough to watch* TOM *open the door the merest crack. She is amused. In a moment, she re-enters with a plate of cookies.)* Help yourself.

TOM. Thanks. *(He takes a cookie, and then sits on the floor, near her chair.)*

LAURA. Are the boys warm enough in the rooms? They shut down the heat so early this spring, I guess they didn't expect this little chill.

TOM. We're fine. But this is nice. *(He indicates low fire in fireplace.)*

LAURA. *(Goes back to her sewing.)* I heard you singing.

TOM. I'm sorry if it bothered you.

LAURA. It was very nice.

TOM. If it ever bothers you, just bang on the radiator.

LAURA. What was the name of the song? It's lovely.

TOM. It's an old French song—"The Joys of Love"— *(He speaks the lyric.)*

> The joys of love
> Are but a moment long.
> The pain of love
> Endures forever.

LAURA. And is that true?

   (TOM shrugs his shoulders.)

You sang as though you knew all about the pains of love.

TOM. And you don't think I do?

LAURA. Well—

TOM. You're right.

LAURA. Only the joys.

TOM. Neither, really.

(TEAPOT whistles off-stage.)

LAURA. Then you're a fake. Listening to you, one would think you knew everything there was to know. *(Rises and goes to next room for tea.)* Anyway, I don't believe it. A boy like you.

TOM. It's true.

LAURA. *(Offstage.)* Aren't you bringing someone to the dance after the play Saturday?

TOM. Yes.

LAURA. Well, there.

TOM. You.

LAURA. *(Reappears in doorway with teapot.)* Me?

Tom. Yes, you're going to be a hostess, aren't you?

Laura. Yes, of course, but—

Tom. As a member of the Committee, I'm taking you. All the Committee drew lots—

Laura. And you lost.

Tom. I won.

Laura. (*A little embarrassed by this.*) Oh— My husband could have taken me. (*She sits down again in her chair.*)

Tom. He's not going to be in town. Don't you remember, Mountain Climbing Club has its final outing this week-end.

Laura. Oh, yes, of course. I'd forgotten.

Tom. He's out a lot on that kind of thing, isn't he?

(Laura *ignores his probing.*)

I hope you're not sorry that I'm to be your escort.

Laura. Why, I'll be honored.

Tom. I'm supposed to find out tactfully and without your knowing it what color dress you'll be wearing.

Laura. Why?

Tom. The Committee will send you a corsage.

Laura. Oh, how nice. Well, I don't have much to choose from, I guess my yellow.

Tom. The boy who's in charge of getting the flowers thinks a corsage should be something like a funeral decoration. So I'm taking personal charge of getting yours.

Laura. Thank you.

Tom. You must have gotten lots of flowers when you were acting in the theatre.

Laura. Oh, now and then. Nothing spectacular.

Tom. I can't understand how a person would give up the theatre to come and live in a school— I'm sorry. I mean, I'm glad you did, but, well—

Laura. If you knew the statistics on unemployed actors, you might understand. Anyway, I was never any great shakes at it.

Tom. I can't believe that.

Laura. Then take my word for it.

Tom. (*After a moment—looking into the fire pretending*

to be casual, but actually touching on his love for LAURA.)
Did you ever do any of Shaw's plays?

LAURA. Yes.

TOM. We got an assignment to read any Shaw play we
wanted. I picked *Candida*.

LAURA. Because it was the shortest?

TOM. *(Laughs.)* No—because it sounded like the one
I'd like the best—one I could understand. Did you ever
play Candida?

LAURA. In stock—a very small stock company, way up
in Northern Vermont.

TOM. Do you think she did right to send Marchbanks
away?

LAURA. Well, Shaw made it seem right. Don't you
think?

TOM. *(Really talking about himself.)* That Marchbanks
sure sounded off a lot. I could never sound off like that,
even if I loved a woman the way he did. She could have
made him seem awfully small if she'd wanted to.

LAURA. Well, I guess she wasn't that kind of woman.
Now stand up. Let's see if this fits. *(She rises with dress in
her hands.)*

TOM. *(Gets up.)* My Dad's going to hit the roof when
he hears I'm playing another girl.

LAURA. I think you're a good sport not to mind. Besides,
it's a good part. Lady Teazle in *The School For Scandal.*

TOM. *(Puts on top of dress.)* It all started when I did
Lady Macbeth last year. You weren't here yet for that.
Lucky you.

LAURA. I hear it was very good.

TOM. You should have read a letter I got from my
father. They printed a picture of me in the Alumni Bul-
letin, in costume. He was plenty peeved about it.

LAURA. He shouldn't have been.

TOM. He wrote me saying he might be up here today on
Alumni Fund business. If he comes over here, and you see
him, don't tell him about this.

LAURA. I won't— What about your mother? Did she
come up for the play? *(She helps him button the dress.)*

TOM. I don't see my mother. Didn't you know? *(He starts to roll up pants legs.)*

LAURA. Why no. I didn't.

TOM. She and my father are divorced.

LAURA. I'm sorry.

TOM. You needn't be. They aren't. I was supposed to hold them together. That was how I happened to come into the world. I didn't work. That's a terrible thing, you know, to make a flop of the first job you've got in life.

LAURA. Don't you ever see her?

TOM. Not since I was five. I was with her till five, and then my father took me away. All I remember about my mother is that she was always telling me to go outside and bounce a ball.

LAURA. *(Handing him skirt of the dress.)* You must have done something before Lady Macbeth. When did you play that character named Grace?

TOM. *(Stiffens.)* I never played anyone called Grace.

LAURA. But I hear the boys sometimes calling you Grace. I thought—

(She notices that he's uncomfortable.)

I'm sorry. Have I said something terrible?

TOM. No.

LAURA. But I have. I'm sorry.

TOM. It's all right. But it's a long story.—Last year over at the movies, they did a revival of Grace Moore in *One Night of Love*— I'd seen the revival before and I guess I talked a lot about how wonderful she was before the picture came.—And I guess I oversold it, or something. But she was wonderful!—Anyway, some of the guys started calling me— Grace. It was my own fault, I guess.

LAURA. Nicknames can be terrible— I remember at one time I was called "Beany"— I can't remember why, now —but I remember it made me mad. *(She adjust the dress a little.)* Hold still a moment. We'll have to let this out around here. *(She indicates the bosom.)* What size do you want to be?

TOM. *(He is embarrassed, but rather nicely—not obvi-*

ously and farcically. In his embarrassment he looks at
LAURA'S *bosom, then quickly away—)* I don't know.
Whatever you think.

LAURA. *(She indicates he is to stand on a small wooden
footstool down Left.)* I should think you would have
invited some girl up to see you act, and then take her to
the dance.

TOM. *(Gets on stool.)* There's nobody I could ask.

LAURA. *(Working on hem of dress.)* What do you mean?

TOM. I don't know any girls, really.

LAURA. Oh, certainly back home—

TOM. Last ten years I haven't been home, I mean really
home. Summers my father packs me off to camps, and the
rest of the time I've been at boarding schools.

LAURA. What about Christmas vacation, and Easter?

TOM. My father gets a raft of tickets to plays and con-
certs, and sends me and my aunt.

LAURA. I see.

TOM. So I mean it when I say I don't know any girls.

LAURA. Your room-mate, Al, knows a lot of girls Why
not ask him to fix you up with a blind date?

TOM. I don't know—I can't even dance. I'm telling you
this so you won't expect anything of me Saturday night.

LAURA. We'll sit out and talk.

TOM. Okay.

LAURA. Or I could teach you how to dance. It's quite
simple.

TOM. *(Flustered.)* You?

LAURA. Why not?

TOM. I mean, isn't a person supposed to go to some sort
of dancing class or something? *(He gets down from footstool.)*

LAURA. Not necessarily. Look, I'll show you how simple
it is— *(She assumes the dancing position.)* Hold your left
hand out this way, and put your right hand around my—
(She stops, as she sees him looking at her.) Oh, now you're
kidding me. A boy your age and you don't know how to
dance.

TOM. I'm not kidding you.

LAURA. Well, then, come on. I had to teach my husband. Put your arm around me. *(She raises her arms.)*

TOM. *(Looks at her a moment, afraid to touch this woman he loves— Then to pass it off.)* We better put it off— We'd look kind of silly, both of us in skirts.

LAURA. All right. Take it off, then— No, wait a minute. Just let me stand off and take a look— *(She walks around him.)* You're going to make a very lovely girl.

TOM. Thank you, ma'am— *(He kids a curtsey, like a girl, and starts out of his costume.)*

(MR. HARRIS, *a good-looking young master, comes in the hallway and starts up to* TOM'S *room. On the landing, he knocks on door.)*

LAURA. I wonder who that is?

TOM. All the other fellows have late afternoon classes.

LAURA. *(Opens the door wider, and looks up the stairs.)* Yes?—Oh, David.

HARRIS. *(Turns and looks down the stairs.)* Oh, hello, Laura.

LAURA. I just was wondering who was coming in.

(TOM *proceeds to get out of the costume.)*

HARRIS. I want to see Tom Lee.

LAURA. He's down here. I'm making his costume for the play.

HARRIS. I wonder if I could see him for a moment?

LAURA. Why yes, of course. Tom, Mr. Harris would like to see you. Do you want to use our study, David? I can go into the living room.

HARRIS. No, thanks. I'll wait for him in his room. Will you ask him to come up? *(He opens the door and goes in.)*

LAURA. *(Is puzzled at his intensity—the urgency in his voice. Comes back in the study.)* Tom, Mr. Harris would like to see you in your room. He's gone along.

TOM. That's funny.

LAURA. Wait a minute—take this up with you, try it on in front of your mirror—see if you can move in it— (*She hands him skirt of costume.*) When Mr. Harris is through, bring the costume back.

TOM. (*Anxious over what HARRIS wants to see him about.*) Yeah, sure. (*He starts out, then stops and picks up a cookie. He looks at her lovingly.*) Thanks for tea.

LAURA. You're welcome.

(TOM *goes to the hall door as* LAURA *turns to the desk. He stands in the door a moment and looks at her back, then he turns and shuts the door and heads upstairs.* HARRIS *has come into* TOM's *bedroom and is standing there nervously clenching and unclenching his hands.*)

TOM. (*Off-stage—presumably in the sitting room he shares with his room-mate.*) Mr. Harris?

(LAURA *wanders off up Right into the other part of the house after looking for a moment at the Canada vacation material on the desk.*)

HARRIS. I'm in here.

TOM. (*Comes in a little hesitantly.*) Oh! Hello, sir.

(HARRIS *closes the door to the bedroom.* TOM *regards this action with some nervousness.*)

HARRIS. Well?

TOM. (*Has dumped some clothes from a chair to his bed. Offers chair to* HARRIS.) Sir?

HARRIS. What did you tell the Dean?

DEAN. What do you mean, Mr. Harris?

HARRIS. What did you tell the Dean?

TOM. When? What are you talking about, sir?

HARRIS. Didn't the Dean call you in?

TOM. No. Why should he?

HARRIS. He didn't call you in and ask you about last Saturday afternoon?

TOM. Why should he? I didn't do anything wrong.

HARRIS. About being with me?

TOM. I'm allowed to leave town for the day in the company of a master.

HARRIS. I don't believe you. You must have said something.

TOM. About what?

HARRIS. About you and me going down to the dunes and swimming.

TOM. Why should I tell him about that?

HARRIS. *(Threatening.)* Why didn't you keep your mouth shut?

TOM. *(Yelling.)* About what? What, for God's sake?

HARRIS. I never touched you, did I?

TOM. What do you mean, touch me?

HARRIS. Did you say to the Dean I touched you?

TOM. *(Turning away from* HARRIS.*)* I don't know what you're talking about.

HARRIS. Here's what I'm talking about. The Dean's had me on the carpet all afternoon. I probably won't be reappointed next year—and all because I took you swimming down off the dunes on Saturday.

TOM. Why should he have you on the carpet for that?

HARRIS. You can't imagine, I suppose.

TOM. What did you do wrong?

HARRIS. Nothing! Nothing, unless you made it seem like something wrong. Did you?

TOM. I told you I didn't see the Dean.

HARRIS. You will. He'll call for you— Bunch of gossiping old busy-bodies!—Well— *(He starts for the door —stops—turns around and softens. He comes back to the puzzled* TOM.*)* I'm sorry— It probably wasn't your fault. It was my fault. I should have been more—discreet— Goodbye. Good luck with your music.

*(*TOM *hasn't understood. He doesn't know what to say.*

He makes a helpless gesture with his hands. HARRIS *goes into the sitting room on his way out.)*

(THREE BOYS, *about 17, come in from the downstairs front door and start up the stairs. They're carrying books.* ALL *are wearing sports jackets, khaki or flannel trousers, white or saddle rubber-soled shoes.)*

AL. I don't believe a word of it.

RALPH. *(He is large and a loud-mouth bully.)* I'm telling you the guys saw them down at the dunes.

AL. *(He is* TOM'S *room-mate—an athlete—clean-cut.)* So what?

RALPH. They were bare-assed.

AL. Shut up, will you? You want Mrs. Reynolds to hear you?

RALPH. Okay. You watch and see. Harris'll get bounced —and I'm gonna lock my room at night as long as Tom is living in this house.

AL. Oh, dry up!

RALPH. Jeeze, you're his room-mate and you're not worried.

HARRIS. *(Comes out the door and starts down the stairs.)* Hello. *(He goes down stairs and out.)*

AL. Sir.

RALPH. Do you believe me now? You aren't safe. Believe me.

STEVE. *(He is small—*RALPH'S *appreciative audience.)* Hey, Al, can I come in and watch Mrs. Morrison nurse her kid?

RALPH. You're the loudest-mouthed bastard I ever heard. You want to give it away.

STEVE. It's time. How about it, Al?

AL. *(Grudgingly.)* Come on.

(TOM *hears them coming and moves to bolt his door, but* STEVE *and* RALPH *break in before he gets to the door. He watches them from the doorway.* STEVE *rushes to the bed and throws himself across it, look-*

ing out the window next to the bed. RALPH *settles down next to him.)*

AL. *(To* TOM *as he comes in.)* Hi— These horny bastards.

STEVE. Al, bring the glasses.

(AL *goes into sitting-room.)*

RALPH. Some day she's going to wean that little bastard and spoil all our fun.

STEVE. Imagine sitting in a window—

TOM. *(Has been watching this with growing annoyance.)* Will you guys get out of here?

RALPH. *(Notices* TOM *for the first time.)* What's the matter with you, Grace?

TOM. This is my damned room.

RALPH. Gracey's getting private all of a sudden.

TOM. I don't want a lot of you peeping-Toms lying on my bed watching a—a—

STEVE. You want it all for yourself, don't you?

RALPH. Or aren't you interested in women?

AL. *(Comes back in with field glasses.)* Shut up! *(Looks out window,—then realizes* TOM *is watching him. Embarrassed.)* These horny bastards.

STEVE. *(Looking.)* Geeze!

RALPH. *(A bully—riding down on* TOM.) I thought you were going to play ball with us Saturday.

TOM. I didn't feel like it.

RALPH. What *did* you feel like doing, huh?

AL. Will you shut up?

STEVE. Hey, lookit. *(Grabs glasses from* AL.)

(AL *leaves room.)*

TOM. *(Climbing over* STEVE *and* RALPH *and trying to pull the shade.)* I told you to get out. I told you last time—

RALPH. *(Grabbing hold of* TOM, *and holding him*

down.) Be still, boy, or she'll see, and you'll spoil everything.

Tom. Horny bastard. Get out of here.

Ralph. Who are you calling a horny bastard? *(He grabs hold of Tom more forcefully, and slaps him a couple of times across the face—not trying to hurt him, but just to humiliate him. Steve gets in a few pokes—and in a moment, it's not in fun, but verging on the serious.)* You don't mean that now, boy, do you? Do you, Grace? *(He slaps him again.)*

Al. *(Hearing the scuffle, comes in, and hauls Ralph and Steve off Tom.)* Come on, come on, break it up. Clear out.

(He has them Both standing up now, Tom still on the bed.)

Ralph. I just don't like that son of a bitch calling me a horny bastard— Maybe if it was Dr. Morrison instead of Mrs. Morrison, he'd be more interested. Hey, wouldn't you, Grace?

(He tries to stick his face in front of Tom, but Al holds him back.)

Al. Come on, lay off the guy, will you? Go on. Get ready for supper. *(He herds them out during this.)*

(When they have left the room, Tom gets up and goes to bureau and gets a handkerchief. He has a bloody nose. He lies down on the bed, his head tilted back to stop the blood.)

Al. *(In doorway.)* You all right?
Tom. Yeah.

(Ralph and Steve go up the stairway singing in raucous voices, "One Night of Love." The downstairs outside door opens, and Bill Reynolds enters the hall

with a student, PHIL. BILL *is* LAURA'S *husband. He
is large and strong with a tendency to be gruff. He's
wearing grey flannel trousers, a tweed jacket, a blue
button-down shirt. He is around 40.)*

BILL. Okay, boy, we'll look forward to— *(He notices*
RALPH *still singing. He goes to the bend in the stairs and
calls.)* Hey, Ralph— Ralph!

RALPH. *(Stops singing up out of sight.)* You calling me,
Mr. Reynolds, sir?

BILL. Yeah. Keep it down to a shout, will you?

RALPH. Oh, *yes, sir.* Sorry, I didn't know I was disturb-
ing you, Mr. Reynolds.

BILL. *(Comes back and talks with* PHIL *at the bend in
stairway.)* Phil, you come on up to the Lodge around—
Let's see— We'll open the Lodge around July first, so
you plan to come up say, July third, and stay for two
weeks— Okay?

PHIL. That'll be swell, sir.

BILL. Frank Hocktor's coming then. You get along with
Frank, don't you? He's a regular guy.

PHIL. Oh, sure.

BILL. The float's all gone to pieces. We can make that
your project to fix it up. Okay?

PHIL. Thanks a lot, Mr. Reynolds. *(He goes on up the
stairs.)*

BILL. See you. *(He comes in and crosses to desk phone
and starts to call.)*

LAURA. *(Offstage.)* Tom?

(BILL *looks around in the direction of the voice, but
says nothing.)*

(Comes on.) Oh, Bill. Tom was down trying on his costume. I thought— You're early.

BILL. Yeah. I want to catch the Dean before he leaves
his office.

(LAURA *goes up to him to be kissed, but he's too
intent on the phone, and she compromises by kissing
his cheek.)*

(In phone.) Hello, this is Mr. Reynolds. Is the Dean still in his office?

LAURA. What's the matter, Bill?

BILL. Nothing very pretty. *(In phone.)* Oh?—How long ago? All right. Thanks. I'll give him a couple of minutes, then I'll call him home. *(Hangs up.)* Well, they finally caught up with Harris. *(He goes into the next room to take off his jacket.)*

LAURA. What do you mean, "caught up" with him?

BILL. *(Offstage.)* You're going to hear it anyhow— so— Last Saturday they caught him down in the dunes, naked.

LAURA. *(Crosses to close door to hall.)* What's wrong with that?

BILL. *(Enters and crosses to fireplace and starts to go through letters propped there. He has taken off his jacket.)* He wasn't alone.

LAURA. Oh!

BILL. He was lying there naked in the dunes, and one of the students was lying there naked too.—Just to talk about it is disgusting.

LAURA. I see.

BILL. I guess you'll admit that's something.

LAURA. I can't see that it's necessarily conclusive.

BILL. With a man like Harris, it's conclusive enough. *(Then casually.)* The student with him was—

LAURA. *(Interrupting.)* I'm not sure I care to know.

BILL. I'm afraid you're going to have to know sooner or later, Laura. It was Tom Lee.

> (TOM *rises from bed, grabs a towel and goes out up the stairs.* LAURA *just looks at* BILL *and frowns.*)

Some of the boys down on the Varsity Club outing came on them—or at least saw them.—And Fin Hadley saw them too, and he apparently used his brains for once and spoke to the Dean.

LAURA. And?

BILL. He's had Harris on the carpet this afternoon.—I guess he'll be fired.—I certainly hope so. Maybe Tom too, I don't know.

LAURA. They put two and two together?

BILL. Yes, Laura.

LAURA. I suppose this is all over school by now.

BILL. I'm afraid so.

LAURA. And most of the boys know.

BILL. Yes.

LAURA. So what's going to happen to Tom?

BILL. *(Takes pipe from mantelpiece and cleans it.)* I know you won't like this, Laura, but I think he should be kicked out. I think you've got to let people know the school doesn't stand for even a hint of this sort of thing. He should be booted.

LAURA. For what?

BILL. Look, a boy's caught coming out of Ellie Martin's rooms across the river. That's enough evidence. Nobody asks particulars. They don't go to Ellie's rooms to play Canasta. It's the same here.

LAURA. *(Hardly daring to suggest it.)* But, Bill—you don't think— I mean, you don't think Tom is— *(She stops.)*

   (BILL *looks at her a moment—his answer is in his silence.)*

Oh, Bill!

BILL. And I'm ashamed and sorry as hell for his father. Herb Lee was always damned good to me—came down from college when I was playing football here—helped me get into college—looked after me when I was in college and he was in law school— *(Crosses to desk.)* And I know he put the boy in my house hoping I could do something with him—*(He dials number.)*

LAURA. And you feel you've failed.

BILL. Yes. *(He pauses.)* With your help, I might say. *(Busy signal. He hangs up.)*

LAURA. How?

BILL. Because, Laura, the boy would rather sit around here and talk with you and listen to music and strum his guitar.

LAURA. Bill, I'm not to blame for everything. Everything's not my fault.

BILL. *(Disregarding this.)* What a lousy thing for Herb. *(He looks at a small picture of team on his desk.)* That's Herb.—He was Graduate Manager of the team when I was a sophomore in college.—He was always the manager of the teams, and he really wanted his son to be there in the center of the picture.

LAURA. Why are you calling the Dean?

BILL. I'm going to find out what's being done.

LAURA. I've never seen you like this before.

BILL. This is something that touches me very closely. The name of the school, its reputation, the reputation of all of us here. I went here and my father before me, and one day I hope our children will come here, when we have them. And, of course, one day I hope to be Headmaster.

LAURA. Let's assume that you're right about Harris. It's a terrible thing to say on the evidence you've got, but let's assume you're right. Does it necessarily follow that Tom—

BILL. —Tom was his friend. Everyone knew that.

LAURA. Harris encouraged him in his music.

BILL. Come on, Laura.

LAURA. What if Tom's room-mate, Al, or some other great big athlete had been out with Harris?

BILL. He wouldn't have been.

LAURA. I'm saying what if he had been? Would you have jumped to the same conclusion?

BILL. It would have been different. Tom's always been an off-horse. And now it's quite obvious why. If he's kicked out, maybe it'll bring him to his senses. But he won't change if nothing's done about it.

(LAURA turns away.)

(BILL starts to look over his mail again.) Anyway, why are you so concerned over what happens to Tom Lee?

LAURA. I've come to know him. You even imply that I am somewhat responsible for his present reputation.

BILL. All right. I shouldn't have said that. But you watch, now that it's out in the open. Look at the way he walks, the way he sometimes stands.

LAURA. Oh, Bill!

BILL. All right, so a woman doesn't notice these things. But a man knows a queer when he sees one. *(He has opened a letter. Reads.)* The book-store now has the book you wanted—"The Rose and The Thorn." What's that?

LAURA. A book of poems.—Do you know, Bill, I'll bet he doesn't even know the meaning of the word—queer.

BILL. What do you think he is?

LAURA. I think he's a nice sensitive kid who doesn't know the meaning of the word.

BILL. He's eighteen, or almost. I don't know.

LAURA. How much did you know at eighteen?

BILL. A lot. *(At the desk he now notices the Canada literature.)* What are these?

LAURA. What?

BILL. These.

LAURA. Oh, nothing.

BILL. *(He throws them in wastebasket, then notices her look.)* Well, they're obviously something. *(He takes them out of wastebasket.)*

LAURA. *(The joy of it gone for her.)* I was thinking we might take a motor trip up there this summer.

BILL. *(Dialling phone again.)* I wish you'd said something about it earlier. I've already invited some of the scholarship boys up to the Lodge.—I can't disappoint them.

LAURA. Of course not.

BILL. If you'd said something earlier.

LAURA. It's my fault.

BILL. It's nobody's fault, it's just— *(In phone.)* Hello, Fitz, Bill Reynolds.—I was wondering if you're going to be in tonight after supper.—Oh— Oh, I see.—Supper? Well, sure I could talk about it at supper.—Well, no, I think I'd better drop over alone.—All right. I'll see you at the house then— Goodbye.

(LAURA looks at him, trying to understand him.) BILL comes to her to speak softly to her. Seeing him come, she holds out her arms to be embraced—but he just takes her chin in his hand.)

Look, Laura, when I brought you here a year ago, I told you it was a tough place for a woman with a heart like yours. I told you you'd run across boys, big and little boys, full of problems, problems which for the moment seem gigantic and heart-breaking. And you promised me then you wouldn't get all taken up with them. Remember?

LAURA. Yes.

BILL. When I was a kid in school here, I had my problems too. There's a place up by the golf course where I used to go off alone Sunday afternoons and cry my eyes out. I used to lie on my bed just the way Tom does, listening to phonograph records hour after hour.

(LAURA, *touched by this, kneels at his side.*)

But I got over it, Laura. I learned how to take it.

(LAURA *looks at him. This touches her.*)

When the Headmaster's wife gave you this tea-pot, she told you what she tells all the new masters' wives. You have to be an interested bystander.

LAURA. I know.

BILL. Just as she said—all you're supposed to do is every once in a while give the boys a little tea and sympathy. Do you remember?

LAURA. Yes, I remember.—It's just that—

BILL. What?

LAURA. This age—seventeen, eighteen. It's so—

BILL. I know.

LAURA. John was this age when I married him.

BILL. —Look, Laura—

LAURA. I know. You don't like me to talk about John, but—

BILL. —It's not that. It's—

LAURA. —He was just this age, eighteen or so, when I married him— We both were.—And I know how this age can suffer. It's a heartbreaking time—no longer a boy— not yet a man— Bill? Bill?

BILL. *(Looks at her awkwardly for a moment—then starts to move off.)* I'd better clean up if I'm going to get to the Dean's for supper. You don't mind, do you?

LAURA. *(Very quietly.)* I got things in for dinner here. But they'll keep.

BILL. *(Awkwardly.)* I'm sorry, Laura. But you understand, don't you? About this business?

(LAURA *shakes her head, "No."*)

(BILL *stands over her, a little put out that she has not understood his reasoning. He starts to say something several times, then stops. Finally he notices the Five and Dime engagement ring around her neck. He touches it.)* You're not going to wear this ring to the dining hall, are you?

LAURA. Why not?

BILL. It was just a gag. It means something to you, but to them—

LAURA. *(Bearing in, but gently.)* Does it mean anything to you, Bill?

BILL. Well, it did, but— *(He stops with a gesture, unwilling to go into it all.)*

LAURA. I think you're ashamed of the night you gave it to me. That you ever let me see you needed help. That night in Italy, in some vague way you cried out—

BILL. What is the matter with you today? *Me* crying out for help. *(He heads for the alcove.)*

(KNOCK on hall door.)

BILL. It's probably Tom.

(LAURA goes to door.)

HERB. *(This is* HERBERT LEE—TOM'S *father. He is a middle-sized man, fancying himself a man of the world and an extrovert. He is dressed as a conservative Boston businessman, but with still a touch of the collegiate in his attire—buttondown shirt, etc.)* Mrs. Reynolds?

LAURA. Yes?

BILL. *(Stopped by the voice, turns.)* Herb! Come in.

HERB. *(Coming in.)* Hiya, Bill. How are you, fella?

BILL. *(Taking his hand.)* I'm fine, Herb.

HERB. *(Poking his finger into* BILL's *chest.)* Great to see you. *(Looks around to* LAURA.) Oh, uh—

BILL. I don't think you've met Laura, Herb. This is Laura. Laura, this is Herb Lee, Tom's father.

HERB. *(Hearty and friendly, meant to put people at their ease.)* Hello, Laura.

LAURA. I've heard so much about you.

HERB. *(After looking at her for a moment.)* I like her, Bill. I like her very much.

(LAURA *blushes, and is a little taken aback by this.)* *(To* LAURA.) What I'd like to know is how did you manage to do it? *(Cuffing* BILL.) I'll bet you make her life miserable.—You look good, Bill.

BILL. You don't look so bad yourself. *(He takes in a notch in his belt.)*

HERB. No, *you're* in shape. I never had anything to keep in shape, but you.—You should have seen this boy, Laura.

LAURA. I've seen pictures.

HERB. Only exercise I get these days is bending the elbow.

LAURA. May I get you something? A drink?

HERB. No, thanks. I haven't got much time.

BILL. You drive out from Boston, Herb?

HERB. No, train. You know, Bill, I think that's the same old train you and I used to ride in when we came here.

BILL. Probably is.

HERB. If I don't catch the six-fifty-four, I'll have to stay all night, and I'd rather not.

BILL. We'd be glad to put you up.

HERB. No. You're putting me up in a couple of weeks at the reunion. That's imposing enough.

(There is an awkward pause. BOTH *men sit down,* BILL *in Right armchair;* HERB *in Left.)*

I—uh—was over at the Dean's this afternoon.

BILL. Oh, he called you?

HERB. Why, no. I was up discussing Alumni Fund matters with him—and— Do you know about it?

BILL. You mean about Tom?

HERB. Yes. *(Looks at* LAURA.)

BILL. Laura knows too. *(He reaches for her to come to him—and he puts his arm around her waist.)*

HERB. Well, after we discussed the Fund, he told me about that. Thought I ought to hear about it from him. Pretty casual about it, I thought.

BILL. Well, that's Fitz.

HERB. What I want to know is, what was a guy like Harris doing at the school?

BILL. I tried to tell them.

HERB. Was there anyone around like that in our day, Bill?

BILL. No. You're right.

HERB. I tried to find the guy. I wanted to punch his face for him. But he's cleared out.—Is Tom around?

LAURA. He's in his room.

HERB. How'd he get mixed up with a guy like that?

BILL. I don't know, Herb—

HERB. I know. I shouldn't ask you. I know. Of course I don't believe Tom was really involved with this fellow. If I believed that, I'd—well, I don't know what I'd do. You don't believe it, do you, Bill?

BILL. Why— *(Looks at* LAURA.)

HERB. *(Cutting in.)* Of course you don't. But what's the matter? What's happened, Bill? Why isn't my boy a regular fellow? He's had every chance to be since he was knee-high to a grasshopper—boys' camps every summer, boarding schools. What do you think, Laura?

LAURA. I'm afraid I'm not the one to ask, Mr. Lee. *(She breaks away from* BILL.)

HERB. He's always been with men and boys. Why doesn't some of it rub off?

LAURA. You see, I feel he's a "regular fellow"—whatever that is.

HERB. You do?

LAURA. If it's sports that matter, he's an excellent tennis player.

HERB. But Laura, he doesn't even play tennis like a regular fellow. No hard drives and cannon ball serves.

He's a cut artist. He can put more damn twists on that ball.

LAURA. He wins. He's the school champion. And isn't he the champion of your club back home?

(TOM *comes down the stairs and enters his bedroom with the costume skirt and towel.*)

HERB. I'm glad you mentioned that—because that's just what I mean. Do you know, Laura, his winning that championship brought me one of my greatest humiliations? I hadn't been able to watch the match. I was supposed to be in from a round of golf in time, but we got held up on every hole.—And when I got back to the locker room, I heard a couple of men talking about Tom's match in the next locker section. And what they said cut me to the quick, Laura. One of them said, "It's a damn shame Tom Lee won the match. He's a good player, all right, but John Batty is such a regular guy." John Batty was his opponent.—Now what pleasure was there for me in that?

BILL. I know what you mean.

HERB. I *want* to be proud of him. My God, that's why I had him in the first place. That's why I took him from his mother when we split up, but— Look, this is a terrible thing to say, but you know the scholarships the University Clubs sponsors for needy kids.

BILL. Sure.

HERB. Well, I contribute pretty heavily to it, and I happened to latch on to one of the kids we help—an orphan— I sort of talk to him like a father, go up to see him at his school once in awhile—and that kid listens to me—and you know what, he's shaping up better than my own son.

(*There is an awkward pause. Upstairs* TOM *has put a record on the phonograph. It starts playing now.*)

BILL. You saw the Dean, Herb?

HERB. Yes.

BILL. And?

HERB. He told me the circumstances. Told me he was confident that Tom was innocently involved. He actually apologized for the whole thing. He did say that some of the faculty had suggested—though he didn't go along with this—that Tom would be more comfortable if I took him out of school. But I'm not going to. He's had nothing but comfort all his life, and look what's happened. My associates ask me what he wants to be, and I tell them he hasn't made up his mind. Because I'll be damned if I'll tell them he wants to be a singer of folksongs.

(TOM *lies on the bed listening to the music.*)

BILL. So you're going to leave him in?

HERB. Of course. Let him stick it out. It'll be a good lesson.

LAURA. Mightn't it be more than just a lesson, Mr. Lee?

HERB. —Oh, he'll take some kidding. He'll have to work extra hard to prove to them he's—well, manly. It may be the thing that brings him to his senses.

LAURA. Mr. Lee, Tom's a very sensitive boy. He's a very lonely boy.

HERB. Why should he be lonely? I've always seen to it that he's been with people—at camps, at boarding schools.

BILL. He's certainly an off-horse, Herb.

HERB. That's a good way of putting it, Bill. An off-horse. Well, he's going to have to learn to run with the other horses. Well, I'd better be going up.

LAURA. Mr. Lee, this may sound terribly naive of me, and perhaps a trifle indelicate.—But I don't believe your son knows what this is all about. Why Mr. Harris was fired—why the boys will kid him.

HERB. You mean— (*Stops.*)

LAURA. I'm only guessing. But I think when it comes

to these boys, we often take too much knowledge for granted. And I think it's going to come as a terrible shock when he finds out what they're talking about. Not just a lesson, a shock.

HERB. I don't believe he's as naive as all that. I just don't. Well— *(He starts for the hall door.)*

BILL. *(Takes* HERB'S *arm and they go into the hall.)* I'm going over to the Dean's for supper, Herb. If you're through with Tom, come by here, and I'll walk you part way to the station.

HERB. All right. *(Stops on the stairs.)* How do you talk to the boys, Bill?

BILL. I don't know.—I just talk to them.

HERB. They're not your sons. I only talked with Tom, I mean, really talked with him, once before. It was after a Sunday dinner and I made up my mind it was time we sat in a room together and talked about important things. He got sick to his stomach. That's a terrible effect to have on your boy— Well, I'll drop down. *(He takes a roll of money from his pocket and looks at it, then starts up the stairs.)*

BILL. *(Coming into his study.)* Laura, you shouldn't try to tell him about his own son. After all, if he doesn't know the boy, who does?

LAURA. I'm sorry.

*(*BILL *exits up Right into the other part of the house, pulling off his tie.* HERB *has gone up the stairs— knocks on the sitting room door.* LAURA *settles down in her chair and eventually goes on with her sewing.)*

AL. *(Inside—calls.)* Come in.

HERB. *(Goes in and shuts the door. Opens* TOM'S *bed- room door and sticks his head in.)* Hello, there.

TOM. *(Looks up from the bed, surprised.)* Oh— Hi—

HERB. I got held up at the Dean's.

TOM. Oh!

(He has risen, and attempts to kiss his father on the

cheek. But his father holds him off with a firm hand-shake.)

HERB. How's everything? You look bushed.

TOM. I'm okay.

HERB. *(Looking at him closely.)* You sure?

TOM. Sure.

HERB. *(Looking around room.)* This room looks smaller than I remember. *(He throws on light switch.)* I used to have the bed over here.—Used to rain in some nights. *(Comes across phonograph.)* This the one I gave you for Christmas?

TOM. Yeah. It works fine.

HERB. *(Turns phonograph off.)* You're neater than I was. My vest was always behind the radiator, or some-where. *(Sees part of dress costume.)* What's this?

TOM. *(Hesitates for a moment—then:)* A costume Mrs. Reynolds made for me. I'm in the play.

HERB. You didn't write about it.

TOM. I know.

HERB. What are you playing? *(Looks at dress.)*

TOM. You know *The School For Scandal.* I'm play-ing Lady Teazle.

HERB. Tom, I want to talk to you. Last time we tried to talk, it didn't work out so well.

TOM. What's up?

HERB. Tom, I'd like to be your friend. I guess there's something between fathers and sons that keeps them from being friends, but I'd like to try.

TOM. *(Embarrassed.)* Sure, Dad. *(He sits on the bed.)*

HERB. Now when you came here, I told you to make friends slowly. I told you to make sure they were the right kind of friends. You're known by the company you keep. Remember I said that?

TOM. Yes.

HERB. And I told you if you didn't want to go out for sports like football, hockey—that was all right with me. But you'd get in with the right kind of fellow if you

managed these teams. They're usually pretty good guys.
You remember.

TOM. Yes.

HERB. Didn't you believe me?

TOM. Yes, I believed you.

HERB. Okay, then let's say you believed me, but you
decided to go your own way. That's all right too, only
you see what it's led to.

TOM. What?

HERB. You made friends with people like this Harris
guy who got himself fired.

TOM. Why is he getting fired?

HERB. He's being fired because he was seen in the
dunes with you.

TOM. Look, I don't—

HERB. —Naked.

TOM. You too?

HERB. So you know what I'm talking about?

TOM. No, I don't.

HERB. You do too know. I heard my sister tell you once.
She warned you about a janitor in the building down the
street.

TOM. *(Incredulous.)* Mr. Harris—?

HERB. Yes. He's being fired because he's been doing a
lot of suspicious things around apparently, and this
finished it. All right, I'll say it plain, Tom. He's a fairy.
A homosexual.

TOM. Who says so?

HERB. Now, Tom—

TOM. —And seeing us on the beach—

HERB. Yes.

TOM. —And what does that make me?

HERB. Listen, I know you're all right.

TOM. Thanks.

HERB. Now wait a minute.

TOM. Look, we were just swimming.

HERB. All right, all right. So perhaps you didn't know.

TOM. What do you mean perhaps?

HERB. It's the school's fault for having a guy like that

around. But it's your fault for being a damned fool in picking your friends.

TOM. So that's what the guys meant.

HERB. You're going to get a ribbing for a while, but you're going to be a man about it and you're going to take it—and you're going to come through much more careful how you make your friends.

TOM. He's kicked out because he was seen with me on the beach, and I'm telling you that nothing, absolutely nothing— Look, I'm going to the Dean and tell him that Harris did nothing, that—

HERB. (Stopping him.) Look, don't be a fool. It's going to be hard enough for you without sticking your neck out, asking for it.

TOM. But, Dad!

HERB. He's not going to be reappointed next year. Nothing you can say is going to change anyone's mind. You got to think about yourself. Now, first of all, get your hair cut.

(TOM looks at father, disgusted.)

Look, this isn't easy for me. Stop thinking about yourself, and give me a break.

(TOM looks up at this appeal.)

I suppose you think it's going to be fun for me to have to live this down back home. It'll get around, and it'll affect me too. So we've got to see this thing through together. You've got to do your part. Get your hair cut. And then— No, the first thing I want you to do is call whoever is putting on this play, and tell them you're not playing this Lady whatever her name is.

TOM. Why shouldn't I play it? It's the best part in the play, and I was chosen to play it.

HERB. I should think you'd have the sense to see why you shouldn't.

TOM. Wait a minute. You mean—do you mean, you think I'm—whatever you call it? Do you, Dad?

HERB. I told you "no."

TOM. But the fellows are going to think that I'm—and Mrs. Reynolds?

HERB. Yes. You're going to have to fight their thinking it. Yes.

(TOM sits on the bed—the full realization of it dawning.)

RALPH. *(Sticks his head around the stairs from upstairs, and yells.)* Hey, Grace—who's taking you to the dance Saturday night? Hey, Grace! *(He disappears again up the stairs.)*
HERB. What's that all about?
TOM. I don't know.

(LAURA, as the noise comes in, rises and goes to door to stop it, but AL comes into the hall and goes upstairs yelling at the BOYS, and LAURA goes back to her chair.)

HERB. *(Looks at his watch.)* Now— Do you want me to stay over? If I'm not going to stay over tonight, I've got to catch the six-fifty-four.
TOM. Stay over?
HERB. Yes. I didn't bring a change of clothes along, but if you want me to stay over—
TOM. Why should you stay over?
HERB. *(Stung a little by this.)* All right. Now come on down to Bill's room and telephone this drama fellow. So I'll know you're making a start of it. And bring the dress.
TOM. I'll do it tomorrow.
HERB. I'd feel better if you did it tonight. Come on. I'm walking out with Bill. And incidentally, the Dean said if the ribbing goes beyond bounds, you know—you're to come to him and he'll take some steps— He's not going to do anything now, because these things take care of themselves—they're better ignored—

(They have BOTH started out of the bedroom, but during the above HERB goes back for the dress. TOM continues out and stands on the stairs looking at the telephone in the hall.)

HERB. *(Comes out of the sitting room—calls back.)* See you, Al. Take good care of my boy here. *(Starts down stairs—stops.)* You need any money?

TOM. No.

HERB. I'm lining you up with a counselor's job at camp this year. If this thing doesn't spoil it. *(Stops.)* You sure you've got enough money to come home?

TOM. Yes, sure. Look Dad, let me call about the play from here. *(He takes receiver off hook.)*

HERB. Why not use Bill's phone. He won't mind. Come on.

(TOM reluctantly puts phone back on hook.)

Look, if you've got any problems, talk them over with Bill—Mr. Reynolds. He's an old friend, and I think he'd tell you about what I'd tell you in a spot— *(Goes into the study.)* Is Bill ready?

LAURA. He'll be right down. How does the costume work?

TOM. I guess it's all right, only—

HERB. I'd like Tom to use your phone if he may—to call whoever's putting on the play. He's giving up the part.

LAURA. Giving up the part?

HERB. Yes. I've—I want him to. He's doing it for me.

LAURA. Mr. Lee, it was a great honor for him to be chosen to play the part.

HERB. Bill will understand. Bill! *(He thrusts costume into* LAURA's *hand and goes off through alcove.)* Bill, what's the number of the man putting on the play. Tom wants to call him.

(LAURA looks at TOM, who keeps his eyes from her. She makes a move towards him, but he takes a step away.)

BILL. *(Offstage.)* Fred Mayberry—326— You ready, Herb?

HERB. *(Offstage.)* Yes. You don't mind if Tom uses your phone, do you?

BILL. Of course not.

HERB. *(Comes in.)* When do you go on your mountain-climbing week-end, Bill?

BILL. *(Comes in.)* This week-end's the outing.

HERB. Maybe Tom could go with you.

BILL. He's on the dance committee, I think. Of course he's welcome if he wants to. Always has been.

HERB. *(Holding out phone to* TOM.*)* Tom.

> (TOM *hesitates to cross to phone. As* LAURA *watches him with concern, he makes a move to escape out the door.)*

Three—two—six.

(TOM *slowly crosses to desk, takes the phone and sits.)*

BILL. Will you walk along with us as far as the dining hall, Laura?

LAURA. I don't think I feel like supper, thanks.

BILL. *(Looks from her to* TOM.*)* What?

HERB. I've got to get along if I want to catch my train.

> (TOM *dials phone.)*

BILL. Laura?

> (LAURA *shakes her head, tight-lipped.)*

HERB. Well, then, goodbye, Laura.—I still like you.

LAURA. Still going to the Dean's, Bill?

BILL. Yes. I'll be right back after supper. Sure you don't want to walk along with us to the dining hall?

> (LAURA *shakes her head.)*

TOM. Busy.

HERB. *(Pats his son's arm.)* Keep trying him. We're in this together. Anything you want?

> (TOM *shakes his head "no."*)

Just remember, anything you want, let me know. *(To* LAURA.*)* See you at reunion time.—This'll all be blown over by then. *(He goes off in hall.)*

BILL. Laura, I wish you'd— Laura! *(He is disturbed*

by her mood. He sees it's hopeless, and goes after HERB, *leaving door open.)*

TOM. *(At phone.)* Hello, Mr. Mayberry— This is Tom Lee.—Yes, I know it's time to go to supper, Mr. Mayberry— *(Looks around at open door.)*

(LAURA *shuts it.)*

but I wanted you to know— *(This comes hard.)* I wanted you to know I'm not going to be able to play in the play— No— I—well, I just can't. *(He is about to break. He doesn't trust himself to speak.)*

LAURA. *(Quickly crosses and takes phone from* TOM.*)* Give it to me. Hello, Fred—Laura. Yes, Tom's father, well, he wants Tom—he thinks Tom is tired, needs to concentrate on his final exams.—You had someone covering the part, didn't you?—Yes, of course it's a terrible disappointment to Tom. I'll see you tomorrow. *(She hangs up.)*

(TOM *is ashamed and humiliated. Here is the woman he loves, hearing all about him—perhaps believing the things.* LAURA *stands above him for a moment, looking at the back of his head with pity. Then he rises and starts for the hall door without looking at her.* RALPH *and* STEVE *come stampeding down the stairway.)*

RALPH. *(As he goes.)* Okay, you can sit next to him if you want. Not me.

STEVE. Well, if you won't—why should I?

RALPH. Two bits nobody will.

(They slam out the front door. TOM *has shut the door quickly again when he has heard* RALPH *and* STEVE *starts down. Now stands against the door listening.)*

AL. *(Comes out from his door, pulling on his jacket. Calls.)* Tom—Tom! *(Getting no answer, he goes down the stairs and out.)*

LAURA. Tom—

TOM. *(Opens the study door.)* I'll bet my father thinks I'm— *(Stops.)*

LAURA. Now, Tom! I thought I'd call Joan Harrison and ask her to come over for tea tomorrow. I want you to come too. I want you to ask her to go to the dance with you.

TOM. *(Turns in anguish and looks at her.)* You were to go with me.

LAURA. I know, but—

TOM. Do you think so too, like the others? Like my father?

LAURA. Tom!

TOM. Is that why you're shoving me off on Joan?

LAURA. *(Moving towards him.)* Tom, I asked her over so that we could lick this thing.

TOM. *(Turns on her.)* What thing? What thing?

(He looks at her a moment, filled with indignation, then he bolts up the stairs. But on the way up, PHIL is coming down. TOM feels like a trapped rat. He starts to turn down the stairs again, but he doesn't want to face LAURA, as he is about to break. He tries to hide his face and cowers along one side going up.)

PHIL. What's the matter with you?

TOM doesn't answer—goes on up and into the sitting room. PHIL shrugs his shoulders and goes on down the stairs and out. TOM comes into his own bedroom and shuts the door and leans against the doorjamb. LAURA goes to the partly opened door. Her impulse is to go up to TOM to comfort him—but she checks self, and turns in the doorway and closes the door, and then walks back to her chair and sits down and reaches out and touches the tea-pot, as though she were half-unconsciously rubbing out a spot. She is puzzled and worried. Upstairs we hear the first few sobs from TOM as the LIGHTS dim out, and

THE CURTAIN FALLS

ACT TWO

Scene I

SCENE: *The scene is the same.*

TIME: *The time is two days later.*

(As the Curtain rises, AL is standing at the hall telephone fastened to the wall on the first landing. He seems to be doing more listening than talking.)

AL. Yeah— *(He patiently waits through a long tirade.)* Yeah, Dad. I know, Dad— No, I haven't done anything about it, yet.—Yes, Mr. Hudson says he has a room in his house for me next year.—But I haven't done anything about it here yet.—Yeah, okay, Dad— I know what you mean. *(Gets angry.)* I swear to God I don't.—I lived with him a year, and I don't.—All right, okay, Dad.—No, don't *you* call. I'll do it. Right now. *(He hangs up. He stands and puts his hands in his pocket and tries to think this out. It's something he doesn't like.)*

RALPH. *(Comes in the front door and starts up the steps.)* Hey, Al?

AL. Yeah?

RALPH. The guys over at the Beta house want to know has it happened yet?

AL. Has what happened?

RALPH. Has Tom made a pass at you yet?

AL. *(Reaches out to swat RALPH.)* For crying out loud!

RALPH. Okay, okay! You can borrow my chastity belt if you need it.

AL. That's not funny.

RALPH. *(Shifting his meaning to hurt AL.)* No, I know it's not. The guys on the ball team don't think it' funny at all.

43

AL. What do you mean?

RALPH. The guy they're supposed to elect captain rooming with a queer.

AL. *(Looks at him for a moment, then rejects the idea.)* Aw—knock it off, huh!

RALPH. So you don't believe me.—Wait and see. *(Putting on a dirty grin.)* Anyway, my mother said I should save myself for the girl I marry. Hell, how would you like to have to tell your wife, "Honey, I've been saving myself for you, except for one night when a guy—"

(AL *roughs* RALPH *up with no intention of hurting him.)*

Okay, okay. So you don't want to be captain of the baseball team. So who the hell cares. I don't. I'm sure.

AL. Look. Why don't you mind your own business?

RALPH. What the hell fun would there be in that?

AL. Ralph, Tom's a nice kid.

RALPH. Yeah. That's why all the guys leave the shower room at the gym when he walks in.

AL. When?

RALPH. Yesterday—today. You didn't hear about it?

AL. No. What are they trying to do?

RALPH. Hell, they don't want some queer looking at them and—

AL. Oh, can it! Go on up and bury your horny nose in your Art Models magazine.

RALPH. At least I'm normal. I like to look at pictures of naked girls—not men, the way Tom does.

AL. Jeeze, I'm gonna push your face in—in a—

RALPH. Didn't you notice all those strong man poses he's got in his bottom drawer?

AL. Yes, I've noticed them. His old man wants him to be a muscle man, and he wrote away for this course in muscle building—and they send those pictures. Any objections?

RALPH. Go on, stick up for him. Stick your neck out. You'll get it chopped off with a baseball bat, you crazy bastard. *(Exits upstairs.)*

(AL *looks at the phone, then up the way* RALPH *went. He is upset. He throws himself into a few push-ups, using the bannisters. Then, still not happy with what he's doing, he walks down the stairs and knocks on the study door.*)

LAURA. (*Comes from the alcove and opens the door.*) Oh, hello, Al.

AL. Is Mr. Reynolds in?

LAURA. Why, no, he isn't. Can I do something?

AL. I guess I better drop down when he's in.

LAURA. All right.—I don't really expect him home till after supper tonight.

AL. (*Thinks for a moment.*) Well—well, you might tell him just so's he'll know and can make other plans.—I won't be rooming in this house next year. This is the last day for changing, and I want him to know that.

LAURA. (*Moves into the room to get a cigarette from Center table.*) I see. Well, I know he'll be sorry to hear that, Al.

AL. I'm going across the street to Harmon House.

LAURA. Both you and Tom going over?

AL. No.

LAURA. Oh!

AL. Just me.

LAURA. I see. Does Tom know this?

AL. No. I haven't told him.

LAURA. You'll have to tell him, won't you, so he'll be able to make other plans.

AL. Yes, I suppose so.

LAURA. Al, won't you sit down for a moment, please? (AL *hesitates, but comes in and sits down.*) (*Offers* AL *a cigarette.*) Cigarette?

AL. (*Reaches for one automatically, then stops.*) No, thanks. I'm in training. (*He slips a pack of cigarettes from his shirt pocket to his trousers pocket.*)

LAURA. That's right. I'm going to watch you play Saturday afternoon.

(AL *smiles at her.*)

You're not looking forward to telling Tom, are you, Al?
    (AL *shakes his head, "No."*)
I suppose I can guess why you're not rooming with him
next year.
    (AL *shrugs his shoulders.*)
I wonder if you know how much it has meant for him
to room with you this year. It's done a lot for him too. It's
given him a confidence to know he was rooming with
one of the big men of the school.

AL. *(Embarrassed.)* Oh—

LAURA. You wouldn't understand what it means to be
befriended. You're one of the strong people. I'm surprised,
Al.

AL. *(Blurting it out.)* My father's called me three
times. How he ever found out about Harris and Tom, I
don't know. But he did. And some guy called him and
asked him, "Isn't that the boy your son is rooming with?"
—and he wants me to change for next year.

LAURA. What did you tell your father?

AL. I told him Tom wasn't so bad, and— Oh, I'd better
wait and see Mr. Reynolds.

LAURA. Al, you've lived with Tom. You know him better than anyone else knows him. If you do this, it's as
good as finishing him so far as this school is concerned—
and maybe farther.

AL. *(Almost whispering it.)* Well, he does act sort of
queer, Mrs. Reynolds. He—

LAURA. —You never said this before. You never paid
any attention before. What do you mean, "queer"?

AL. Well, like the fellows say, he sort of walks lightly,
if you know what I mean. Sometimes the way he moves—
the things he talks about—long-hair music all the time.

LAURA. All right. He wants to be a singer. So he talks
about it.

AL. He's never had a girl up for any of the dances.

LAURA. Al, there are good explanations for all these
things you're saying. They're silly—and prejudiced—and
arguments all dug up to suit a point of view. They're all
after the fact.

AL. I'd better speak to Mr. Reynolds. *(He starts for the door.)*

LAURA. Al, look at me. *(She holds his eyes for a long time, wondering whether to say what she wants to say--)*

AL. Yes?

LAURA. *(She decides to do it.)* Al, what if I were to start the rumor tomorrow that you were—well, queer, as you put it?

AL. No one would believe it.

LAURA. Why not?

AL. Well, because—

LAURA. Because you're big and brawny and an athlete. What they call a top guy and a hard hitter?

AL. Well, yes.

LAURA. You've got some things to learn, Al. I've been around a little, and I've met men, just like you—same set-up—who weren't men, some of them married and with children.

AL. Mrs. Reynolds, you wouldn't do a thing like that.

LAURA. No, Al, I probably wouldn't. But I could, and I almost would to show you how easy it is to smear a person, and once I got them believing it, you'd be surprised how quickly your—manly virtues would be changed into suspicious characteristics.

AL. *(Has been standing with his hands on his hips.* (LAURA *looks pointedly at this stance.)*
(AL *thrusts his hands down to his side, and then behind his back.)* Mrs. Reynolds, I got a chance to be captain of the baseball team next year.

LAURA. I know. And I have no right to ask you to give up that chance. But I wish somehow or other you could figure out a way—so it wouldn't hurt Tom.

(TOM *comes in the hall and goes up the stairs. He's pretty broken up, and mad. After a few moments he appears in his room, shuts the door, and sits on the bed, trying to figure something out.)*

AL. *(As* TOM *enters house.)* Well—

LAURA. That's Tom now.

(AL, *looks at her wondering how she knows.*)

I know all your footsteps. He's coming in for tea.

(AL *starts to move to door.*)

Well, Al?

(AL *makes a helpless motion.*)

You still want me to tell Mr. Reynolds about your moving next year?

AL. *(After a moment.)* No.

LAURA. Good.

AL. I mean, I'll tell him when I see him.

LAURA. Oh!

AL. *(Turns on her.)* What can I do?

LAURA. I don't know.

AL. Excuse me for saying so, but it's easy for you to talk the way you have—you're not involved. You're just a bystander. You're not going to be hurt. Nothing's going to happen to you one way or the other— I'm sorry.

LAURA. That's a fair criticism, Al. I'm sorry I asked you. As you say, I'm not involved.

AL. I'm sorry. I think you're swell, Mrs. Reynolds. You're the nicest housemaster's wife I've ever run into— I mean— Well, you know what I mean. It's only that— *(He is flustered. He opens the door.)* I'm sorry.

LAURA. I'm sorry, too, Al. *(She smiles at him.)*

(AL *stands in the doorway for a mement, not knowing whether to go out the front door or go upstairs. Finally, he goes upstairs, and in the sitting room.* LAURA *stands thinking over what* AL *has said, even repeating to herself, "I'm not involved." She then goes into the alcove and off.*)

AL. *(Outside* TOM's *bedroom door.)* Tom?

(TOM *moves quietly away from the door.*)

Tom? *(Opens the door.)* Hey.

TOM. I was sleeping.

AL. Standing up, huh?

(TOM *turns away.*)

You want to be alone?

Tom. No. You want to look. Go ahead. *(He indicates the window.)*

Al. No, I don't want to look, I— *(He looks at* Tom, *not knowing how to begin—he stalls—smiling.)* Nice tie you got there.

Tom. *(Starts to undo tie.)* Yeah, it's yours. You want it.

Al. No. Why? I can only wear one tie at a time.

> *(*Tom *leaves it hanging around his neck. After an awkward pause.)*

I—uh—

Tom. I guess I don't need to ask you what's the matter?

Al. It's been rough today, huh?

Tom. Yeah. *(He turns away, very upset—he's been holding it in—but here's his closest friend asking him to to open up.)* Jesus Christ!

> *(*Al *doesn't know what to say. He goes to* Tom's *bureau and picks up his hair brush, gives his hair a few brushes.)*

Anybody talk to you?

Al. Sure. You know they would.

Tom. What do they say?

Al. *(Yanks his tie off.)* Hell, I don't know.

Tom. I went to a meeting of the dance committee. I'm no longer on the dance committee. Said that since I'd backed out of playing the part in the play, I didn't show the proper spirit. That's what they *said* was the reason.

Al. Why the hell don't you do something about it?

Tom. *(Yelling back.)* About what?

Al. About what they're saying.

Tom. What the hell can I do?

Al. Geez, you could— *(He suddenly wonders what* Tom *could do.)* I don't know.

Tom. I tried to pass it off. Christ, you can't pass it off. You know, when I went into the showers today after my tennis match, everyone who was in there, grabbed a towel and—and—walked out.

Al. They're stupid. Just a bunch of stupid bastards. *(He leaves the room.)*

Tom. *(Following him into sitting room.)* Goddamn it, the awful thing I found myself— Jesus, I don't know— I found myslf self-conscious about things I been doing for years. Dressing, undressing— I keep my eyes on the floor— *(Re-enters his own room.)* Geez, if I even look at a guy that doesn't have any clothes on, I'm afraid someone's gonna say something, or— Jesus, I don't know.

Al. *(During this, Al has come back into the room taking off his shirt, unbuttoning it, etc. Suddenly he stops.)* What the hell am I doing? I've had a shower today. *(He tries to laugh.)*

Tom. Undress in your own room, will ya? You don't want them talking about you too. Do you?

Al. No I don't. *(He said this very definitely and with meaning.)*

Tom. *(Looks up at his tone of voice.)* Of course you don't. *(He looks at Al a long time. He hardly dares say this.)* You—uh—you moving out? '

Al. *(Doesn't want to answer.)* Look, Tom, do you mind if I try to help you?

Tom. Hell, no. How?

Al. I know this is gonna burn your tail, and I know it sounds stupid as hell. But it isn't stupid. It's the way people look at things. You could do a lot for yourself, just the way you talk and look.

Tom. You mean get my hair cut?

Al. For one thing.

Tom. Why the hell should a man with a crew cut look more manly than a guy who—

Al. —Look, I don't know the reasons for these things. It's just the way they are.

Tom. *(Looking at himself in bureau mirror.)* I tried a crew cut a coupla times. I haven't got that kind of hair, or that kind of head. *(After a moment.)* Sorry, I didn't mean to yell at you. Thanks for trying to help.

(Al finds a baseball on the radiator and throws it at Tom. Tom smiles, and throws it back.)

AL. Look, Tom, the way you walk—

TOM. Oh! Jesus!

AL. *(Flaring.)* Look, I'm trying to help you.

TOM. No one gave a goddamn about how I walked till last Saturday!

AL. *(Starts to go.)* Okay, okay. Forget it. *(He goes out.)*

TOM. *(Stands there a few moments, then slams the baseball into the bed and walks out after AL into sitting room.)* Al?

AL. *(Off.)* Yeah?

TOM. Tell me about how I walk.

AL. *(In the sitting room.)* Go ahead, walk!

TOM. *(Walks back into the bedroom.)*

> *(AL follows him wiping his face on a towel and watching TOM walk. After he has walked a bit—)*

Now I'm not going to be able to walk any more. Everything I been doing all my life makes me look like a fairy.

AL. Go on.

TOM. All right, now I'm walking. Tell me.

AL. Tom, I don't know. You walk sort of light.

TOM. Light? *(He looks at himself take a step.)*

AL. Yeah.

TOM. Show me.

AL. No, I can't do it.

TOM. Okay. You walk. Let me watch you. I never noticed how you walked.

> *(AL stands there for a moment, never having realized before how difficult it could be to walk if you think about it. Finally he walks.)*

Do it again .

AL. If you go telling any of the guys about this—

TOM. Do you think I would?

> *(AL walks again.)*

That's a good walk. I'll try to copy it. *(He tries to copy the walk, but never succeeds in taking even a step.)* Do you really think that'll make any difference?

AL. *I dunno.*

TOM. Not now it won't. Thanks anyway.

AL. *(Comes and sits on bed beside* TOM. *Puts his arm around* TOM'S *shoulder and thinks this thing out.)* Look, Tom— You've been in on a lot of bull sessions. You heard the guys talking about stopping over in Boston on the way home—getting girls—you know.

TOM. Sure. What about it?

AL. You're not going to the dance Saturday night?

TOM. No. Not now.

AL. You know Ellie Martin. The gal who waits on table down at the soda joint?

TOM. Yeah. What about her?

AL. You've heard the guys talking about her.

TOM. Come on, come on.

AL. Why don't you drop in on Ellie Saturday night?

TOM. What do you mean?

AL. Hell, do you want me to draw a picture?

TOM. Ellie Martin?

AL. Okay. I know she's a dog, but—

TOM. So what good's that going to do? I get caught there, I get thrown out of school.

AL. No one ever gets caught. Sunday morning people'd hear about—not the Dean— I mean the fellows. Hell, Ellie tells and tells and tells— Boy, you'd be made!

TOM. Are you kidding?

AL. No.

TOM. *(With disgust.)* Ellie Martin!

AL. Look, I've said so much already, I might as well be a complete bastard. You ever been with a woman?

TOM. What do you think?

AL. I don't think you have.

TOM. So?

AL. You want to know something?

TOM. What?

AL. Neither have I. But if you tell the guys, I'll murder you.

TOM. All those stories you told—

AL. —Okay, I'll be sorry I told you.

TOM. Then why don't you go see Ellie Martin Saturday night?

AL. Why the hell should I?

TOM. You mean you don't have to prove anything?

AL. Aw, forget it. It's probably a lousy idea anyway. *(He starts out.)*

TOM. Yeah.

AL. *(Stops.)* Look, about next— *(Stops.)*

TOM. Next year? Yes?

AL. Hap Hudson's asked me to come to his house. He's got a single there. A lot of the fellows from the team are over there, and—well— *(He doesn't look at* TOM.*)*

TOM. Sure, sure— I understand.

AL. Sorry I didn't tell you till now, after we'd made our plans. But I didn't know. I mean, I just found out about the—the opening.

TOM. I understand!

AL. *(Looks up at last. He hates himself but he's done it, and it's a load off his chest.)* See ya. *(He starts to go.)*

TOM. *(As* AL *gets to door.)* Al—

     *(*AL *stops and looks back.)*

(Taking tie from around his neck.) Here.

AL. I said wear it. Keep it.

TOM. It's yours.

AL. *(Looks at the tie for a long time—then without taking it, goes through the door.)* See ya.

*(*TOM *folds the tie neatly, dazed, then seeing what he's doing, he throws it viciously in the direction of the bureau, and turns and stares out the window. He puts a record on the phonograph.)*

BILL. *(Comes in to the study from the hall, carrying a pair of shoes and a slim book. As he opens his door, he hears the music upstairs. He stands in the door and listens, remembering his miserable boyhood. Then he comes in and closes the door.)* Laura.

LAURA. *(Off-stage—calling.)* Bill?

BILL. Yes.

LAURA. *(Coming in with tea things.)* I didn't think you'd be back before your class. Have some tea.

BILL. I beat young Harvey at handball.

LAURA. Good.

BILL. At last. It took some doing, though. He was after my scalp because of that D-minus I gave him in his last exam. *(Gives her book.)* You wanted this—book of poems.

LAURA. *(Looks at book—her eyes shift quickly to the same book in the chair.)* Why yes. How did you know?

BILL. *(Trying to be very off-hand about it.)* The notice from the book-store.

LAURA. That's very nice of you.

(She moves towards him to kiss him—but at this moment, in picking some wrapping paper from the armchair, he notices the duplicate copy.)

BILL. *(A little angry.)* You've already got it.

LAURA. Why, yes— I—well, I—

 (BILL picking it up—opens it.)

That is, someone gave it to me.

 (BILL reads the inscription.)

Tom knew I wanted it, and—

BILL. *(Slowly rips the book in two and hurls it into the fireplace.)* Damn!

LAURA. Bill!

 (BILL goes to ottoman and sits down and begins to changes his shoes.)

Bill, what difference does it make that he gave me the book? He knew I wanted it too.

BILL. I don't know. It's just that every time I try to do something—

LAURA. Bill, how can you say that? It isn't so.

BILL. It is.

LAURA. Bill, this thing of the book is funny.

BILL. I don't think it's very funny.

LAURA. *(Going behind him, and kneeling by his side.)* Bill I'm very touched that you should have remembered. Thank you.

 (He turns away from her and goes on with his shoes.)

Bill, don't turn away. I want to thank you. *(As she gets*

no response from him, she rises.) Is it such a chore to let yourself be thanked? *(She puts her hands on his shoulders, trying to embrace him.)* Oh, Bill, we so rarely touch any more. I keep feeling I'm losing contact with you. Don't you feel that?

BILL. *(Looking at his watch.)* Laura, I—

LAURA. *(She backs away from him.)* I know, you've got to go. But it's just that, I don't know, we don't touch any more. It's a silly way of putting it, but you seem to hold yourself aloof from me. A tension seems to grow between us—and then when we do—touch—it's a violent thing— almost a compulsive thing.

(BILL *is uncomfortable at this accurate description of their relationship. He sits troubled.)*
(Puts her arms around his neck and embraces him, bending over him.) You don't feel it? You don't feel yourself holding away from me until it becomes overpowering? There's no growing together anymore—no quiet times just holding hands, the feeling of closeness, like it was in Italy. Now it's long separations and then this almost brutal coming together, and— Oh, Bill, you do see, you do see.

(BILL *suddenly straightens up, toughens, and looks at her.* LAURA *repulsed, slowly draws her arms from around his shoulders.)*

BILL. For God's sake, Laura, what are you talking about? *(He rises and goes to his desk.)* It can't always be a honeymoon.

(Upstairs in his room, TOM *turns off the phonograph, and leaves the room, going out to the landing and up the stairs.)*

LAURA. Do you think that's what I'm talking about?

BILL. I don't know why you chose a time like this to talk about things like—

LAURA. —I don't know why, either. I just wanted to

thank you for the book— *(Moves away and looks in book.)* What did you write in it?

BILL. *(Starts to mark exam papers.)* Nothing. Why? Should I write in it? I just thought you wanted the book.

LAURA. Of course. Are you sure you won't have some tea? *(She bends over the tea things.)*

BILL. Yes.

LAURA. *(Straigthening up, trying another tack of returning to normality.)* Little Joan Harrison is coming over for tea.

BILL. No, she isn't.

    (LAURA *looks inquiringly.)*

I just saw her father at the gym. I don't think that was a very smart thing for you to do, Laura.

LAURA. I thought Tom might take her to the dance Saturday. He's on the committee, and he has no girl to take.

BILL. I understand he's no longer on the committee. You're a hostess, aren't you?

LAURA. Yes.

BILL. I've got the mountain climbing business this weekend. Weather man predicts rain.

LAURA. *(Almost breaks. Hides her face in her hands. Then recovers.)* That's too bad. *(After a moment.)* Bill?

BILL. Yes?

LAURA. I think someone should go to the Dean about Tom and the hazing he's getting.

BILL. What could the Dean do? Announce from chapel, "you've got to stop riding Tom. You've got to stop calling him 'Grace' "? Is that what you'd like him to do?

LAURA. No. I suppose not.

BILL. You know we're losing Al next year because of Tom.

LAURA. Oh, you've heard?

BILL. Yes, Hudson tells me he's moving over to his house. He'll probably be captain of the baseball team. Last time we had a major sport captain was eight years ago.

LAURA. Yes, I'm sorry.

BILL. However, we'll also be losing Tom

LAURA. Oh?

BILL. *(Noting her increased interest.)* Yes. We have no singles in this house, and he'll be rooming alone.

LAURA. I'm sorry to hear that.

BILL. *(He turns to look at her.)* I knew you would be.

LAURA. Why should my interest in this boy make you angry?

BILL. I'm not angry.

LAURA. You're not only angry. It's almost as though you were, well, jealous.

BILL. Oh, come on now.

LAURA. Well, how else can you explain your—your vindictive attitude towards him?

BILL. Why go into it again? Jealous! *(He has his books together now—goes to hall door.)* I'll go directly from class to the dining hall. All right?

LAURA. Yes, of course.

BILL. And please, please, Laura— *(He stops.)*

LAURA. I'll try.

BILL. I know you like to be different, just for the sake of being different—and I like you for that.—But this time, lay off. Show your fine free spirit on something else.

LAURA. On something that can't hurt us?

BILL. All right. Sure. I don't mind putting it that way— And, Laura?

LAURA. Yes?

BILL. Seeing Tom so much—having him down for tea alone all the time—

LAURA. Yes?

BILL. I think you should have him down only when you have the other boys—for his own good. I mean that. Well, I'll see you in the dining hall. Try to be in time. *(He goes out.)*

> (LAURA *brings her hands to her face, and cries, leaning against the back of the chair.* AL *has come tumbling out of the door to his room with books in hand, and is coming down the stairs.)*

(Going down the hall.) You going to class, Al?

AL. Hello, Mr. Reynolds. Yes I am.

BILL. *(As they go.)* Let's walk along together— I'm

sorry to hear that you're moving across the street next year. *(And they are gone out the door.)*

TOM. *(Has come down the stairs, and now stands looking at the hall telephone. He is carrying his coat. After a long moment's deliberation, he puts in a coin and dials.)* Hello, I'd like to speak to Ellie Martin, please.

> *(LAURA has moved to pick up the torn book which her husband has thrown in the fireplace. She is smoothing it out, as she suddenly hears TOM's voice in the hall. She can't help but hear what he is saying. She stands stock still and listens, her alarm and concern showing in her face.)*

Hello, Ellie? This is Tom Lee— Tom Lee. I'm down at the soda fountain all the time with my roommate, Al Thomson— Yeah, the guys do sometimes call me that— Well, I'll tell you what I wanted. I wondered if—you see, I'm not going to the dance Saturday night, and I wondered if you're doing anything?—Yeah, I guess that is a hell of a way to ask for a date—but I just wondered if I could maybe drop by and pick you up after work on Saturday. —I don't know what's in it for you, Ellie—but something, I guess. I just thought I'd like to see you— What time do you get through work?—Okay, nine o'clock.

> *(LAURA, having heard this, goes out through the alcove.)*

(About to hang up.) Oh, thanks. *(He stands for a moment, contemplating what he's done, then he slips on his jacket, and goes to the study door and knocks. After a moment, he opens the door and enters.)*

LAURA. *(Coming from the other room with a plate of cookies.)* Oh, there you are— I've got your favorites today.

TOM. Mrs. Reynolds, do you mind if I don't come to tea this afternoon?

LAURA. Why—if you don't want to.—How are you? *(She really means this question.)*

TOM. I'm okay?

LAURA. Good.

TOM. It's just I don't feel like tea.

LAURA. Perhaps, it's just as well. Joan can't make it today, either.

TOM. I didn't expect she would.—She's nothing special; just a kid.

LAURA. Something about a dentist appointment or something.

TOM. It wouldn't have done any good anyway. I'm not going to the dance.

LAURA. Oh?

TOM. Another member of the committee will stop around for you.

LAURA. What will you be doing?

TOM. I don't know. I can take care of myself

LAURA. If you're not going, that gives me an easy out. I won't have to go.

TOM. Just because I'm not going.

LAURA. Look, Tom—now that neither of us is going, why don't you drop down here after supper, Saturday night.—We could listen to some records, or play gin, or we can just talk.

TOM. I— I don't think you'd better count on me.

LAURA. I'd like to.

TOM. No, really. I don't want to sound rude—but I— I may have another engagement.

LAURA. Oh!

TOM. I'd like to come. Please understand that. It's what I'd like to do—but—

LAURA. Well, I'll be here—just in case you decide to come in. (LAURA *extends her hand.*) I hope you'll be feeling better.

TOM. (*Hesitates, then takes her hand.*) Thanks.

LAURA. Maybe your plans will change.

(TOM *looks at her—wishing they would; knowing they won't. He runs out and down the hall as the LIGHTS fade out on* LAURA *standing at the door.*)

CURTAIN

ACT TWO

SCENE II

The time is eight-forty-five on Saturday night.

In the study a low fire is burning. As the Curtain rises, the town clock is striking the three quarter hour. LAURA is sitting in her chair sipping a cup of coffee. The door to the study is open slightly. She is waiting for TOM. She is wearing a single flower. In his room, TOM listens to the clock strike. He has just been shaving. He is putting shaving lotion on his face. His face is tense and nervous. There is no joy in the preparations. In a moment, he turns and leaves the room, taking off his belt as he goes.

After a moment, LILLY comes to the study door, knocks and comes in.

LILLY. Laura?

LAURA. Oh, Lilly

LILLY. *(Standing in the doorway, a raincoat held over her head. She is dressed in a low cut evening gown, which she wears very well.)* You're not dressed yet. Why aren't you dressed for the dance?

LAURA. *(Still in her chair.)* I'm not going. I thought I told you.

LILLY. *(Deposits raincoat and goes immediately to look at herself in mirror next to the door.)* Oh, for Heaven's sake, why not? Just because Bill's away with his loathesome little mountain climbers.

LAURA. Well—

LILLY. Come along with us. It's raining on and off, so Harry's going to drive us in the car.

LAURA. No, thanks.

LILLY. If you come, Harry will dance with you all evening. You won't be lonely, I promise you.

(LAURA shakes her head, "no.")

You're the only one who can dance those funny steps with him.

LAURA. It's very sweet of you, but no.

LILLY. *(At the mirror.)* Do you think this neck is too low?

LAURA. I think you look lovely.

LILLY. Harry says this neck will drive all the boys crazy.

LAURA. I don't think so.

LILLY. Well, that's not very flattering.

LAURA. I mean, I think they'll appreciate it but as for driving them crazy—

LILLY. After all I want to give them some reward for dancing their duty dances with me.

LAURA. I'm sure when they dance with you, it's no duty, Lilly. I've seen you at these dances.

LILLY. It's not this— *(Indicating her bosom.)* its my line of chatter. I'm oh so interested in what courses they're taking, where they come from, and where they learned to dance so divinely.

LAURA. *(Laughing.)* Lilly, you're lost in a boy's school. You were meant to shine someplace much more glamorous.

LILLY. I wouldn't trade it for the world. Where else could a girl indulge in three hundred innocent flirtations a year?

LAURA. Lilly, I've often wondered what you'd do if one of the three hundred attempted to go, well, a little further than innocent flirtation.

LILLY. I'd slap him down—the little beast. *(She laughs and admires herself in mirror.)* Harry says if I'm not careful I'll get to looking like Ellie Martin. You've seen Ellie.

LAURA. I saw her this afternoon for the first time.

LILLY. Really? The first time?

LAURA. Yes. I went into the place she works—the soda shop—

LILLY. You!

LAURA. Yes—uh—for a package of cigarettes. *(After a moment she says with some sadness.)* She's not even pretty, is she?

LILLY. *(Turns from admiring herself at the tone in*

LAURA's *voice.)* Well, honey, don't sound so sad. What difference should it make to you if she's pretty or not?

LAURA. I don't know. It just seems so—they're so young.

LILLY. If they're stupid enough to go to Ellie Martin, they deserve whatever happens to them. Anyway, Laura, the boys *talk* more about Ellie than anything else. So don't fret about it.

LAURA. *(Arranges chair for* TOM *facing fireplace—notices* LILLY *primping.)* You look lovely, Lilly.

LILLY. Maybe I'd better wear that corsage the dance committee sent, after all—right here. *(She indicates low point in dress.)*

(LAURA *shrugs.)*

I was going to carry it—or rather Harry was going to help me carry it. You know, it's like one of those things people put on Civil War monuments on Decoration Day.

LAURA. Yes, I've seen them.

LILLY. *(Indicating the flower* LAURA *is wearing.)* Now that's tasteful. Where'd you get that?

LAURA. Uh— I bought it for myself.

LILLY. Oh, now.

LAURA. It's always been a favorite of mine—and I saw it in the florist's window.

LILLY. Well, Harry will be waiting for me to tie his bow tie. *(Starts towards door.)* Will you be up when we get back?

LAURA. *(Giving* LILLY *her raincoat.)* Probably not.

LILLY. If there's a light on, I'll drop in and tell you how many I had to slap down.—Night-night. *(She leaves.)*

(LAURA *stands at the closed door until she hears the outside door close—then she opens her door a bit. She takes her cup of coffee and stands in front of the fireplace and listens.)*

TOM. *(As* LILLY *goes, he returns to his room, dressed in a blue suit. He stands there deliberating a moment, then reaches under his pillow and brings out a pint bottle of whiskey. He takes a short swig. It gags him. He corks it and puts it back under the pillow.)* Christ, I'll never make it. *(He reaches in his closet and pulls out a raincoat, then turns and snaps out the room light, and goes out. A moment later, he appears on the stairs. He see's* LAURA's *door partly open, and while he is putting on his raincoat, he walks warily past it.)*

LAURA. *(When she hears* TOM's *door close, she stands still and listens more intently. She hears him pass her door and go to the front door. She puts down the cup of coffee, and goes to the study door. She calls.)* Tom?

(After some moments, TOM *appears in the door.)* *(She opens it wide.)* I've been expecting you.

TOM. I— I—

LAURA. Are you going to the dance, after all?

TOM. *(Comes to the door.)* No.—You can report me if you want. Out after hours. Or— *(He looks up at her finally.)* Or you can give me permission. Can I have permission to go out?

LAURA. *(Moving into the room, towards the up Right doorsill pleasantly.)* I think I'd better get you some coffee.

TOM. *(At her back, truculent.)* You can tell them that, too—that I've been drinking. There'll be lots to tell before— *(He stops.)*— I didn't drink much. But I didn't eat much either.

LAURA. Let me get you something to eat.

TOM. *(As though convincing himself.)* No. I can't stay!

LAURA. All right. But I'm glad you dropped in. I was counting on it.

TOM. *(Chip on shoulder.)* I said I might not. When you invited me.

LAURA. I know. *(She looks at him a moment. He is to her a heartbreaking sight—all dressed up as though he were going to a prom, but instead he's going to* ELLIE—*the innocence and the desperation touch her deeply, and this shows in her face as she circles behind him to the door.)* It's a nasty night out, isn't it?

Tom. Yes.

Laura. I'm just as glad I'm not going to the dance. *(She shuts the door gently.)*

(Tom, at the sound of the door, turns and sees what she has done.)

It'll be nice just to stay here by the fire.

Tom. I wasn't planning to come in.

Laura. Then why the flower—and the card. "For a pleasant evening?"

Tom. It was for the dance. I forgot to cancel it.

Laura. I'm glad you didn't.

Tom. Why? *(He stops studying the curtains Right, and looks at her.)*

Laura. *(Moving into the room again.)* Well, for one thing I like to get flowers. For another thing—

(Tom shakes his head a little to clear it.)

Let me make you some coffee.

Tom. No. I'm just about right.

Laura. Or you can drink this— I just had a sip. *(She holds up the cup.)*

(Tom looks at the proffered coffee.)

You can drink from this side. *(She indicates the other side of the cup.)*

Tom. *(Takes the cup, and looks at the side where her lips have touched—and then slowly turns it around to the other side and takes a sip.)* And for another thing?

Laura. What do you mean?

Tom. For one thing you like to get flowers—

Laura. For another it's nice to have flowers on my anniversary.

Tom. Anniversary?

Laura. Yes.

Tom. *(Waving the cup and saucer around.)* And Mr. Reynolds on a mountain-top with twenty stalwart youths, soaking wet. Didn't he remember?

Laura. *(Rescues the cup and saucer.)* It's not that anniversary.

(TOM *looks at her wondering.*)
(*Seeing that she has interested him, she moves towards him.*) Let me take your coat.

TOM. (*Definitely.*) I can't——

LAURA. —I know. You can't stay. But—
(*She comes up behind him and puts her hand on his shoulders to take off his coat. He can hardly stand her touch. She gently peels his coat from him and stands back to look at him.*) How nice you look!

TOM. (*Disarranging his hair or tie.*) Put me in a blue suit and I look like a kid.

LAURA. How did you know I liked this flower?

TOM. You mentioned it.

LAURA. You're very quick to notice these things. So was he.

TOM. (*After a moment. His curiosity aroused.*) Who?

LAURA. My first husband. That's the anniversary.

TOM. I didn't know.

LAURA. (*Sits in her chair.*) Mr. Reynolds doesn't like me to talk about my first husband— He was, I'd say, about your age. How old are you, Tom?

TOM. Eighteen—tomorrow.

LAURA. Tomorrow— We must celebrate.

TOM. You'd better not make any plans.

LAURA. He was *just* your age then. (*She looks at him again with slight wonder.*) It doesn't seem possible now, looking at you—

TOM. Why, do I look like such a child?

LAURA. Why no.

TOM. Men are married at my age.

LAURA. Of course, they are. *He* was. Maybe a few months older. Such a lonely boy, away from home for the first time—and—and going off to war.
(TOM *looks up inquiringly.*)
Yes, he was killed.

TOM. I'm sorry—but I'm glad to hear about him.

LAURA. Glad?

TOM. Yes. I don't know— He sounds like someone you

should have been married to, not— *(Stops.)* I'm sorry if
I— *(Stops.)*

LAURA. *(After a moment.)* He was killed being conspicuously brave. He had to be conspicuously brave, you see,
because something had happened in training camp— I
don't know what—and he was afraid the others thought
him a coward.—He showed them he wasn't.

TOM. He had that satisfaction.

LAURA. What was it worth if it killed him?

TOM. I don't know. But I can understand.

LAURA. Of course you can. You're very like him.

TOM. Me?

LAURA. *(Holding out the coffee cup.)* Before I finish it
all?

(TOM *comes over and takes a sip from his side of the
cup.)*

He was kind and gentle, and lonely.

(TOM *turns away in embarrassment at hearing himself described.)*

We knew it wouldn't last.—We sensed it.—But he always
said, "Why must the test of everything be its durability?"

TOM. I'm sorry he was killed.

LAURA. Yes, so am I. I'm sorry he was killed the way he
was killed—trying to prove how brave he was. In trying
to prove he was a man, he died a boy.

TOM. Still he must have died happy.

LAURA. Because he proved his courage?

TOM. That—and because he was married to you. *(Embarrassed, he walks to his coat which she has been holding
in her lap.)* I've got to go.

LAURA. Tom, please.

TOM. I've got to. *(Crosses to door.)*

LAURA. It must be a very important engagement.

TOM. It is.

LAURA. If you go now, I'll think I bored you, talking all
about myself.

TOM. You haven't.

LAURA. I probably shouldn't have gone on like that. It's
just that I felt like it—a rainy Spring night—a fire. I

guess I'm in a reminiscent mood. Do you ever get in reminiscing moods on nights like this?

Tom. About what?

Laura. Oh, come now—there must be something pleasant to remember, or someone.

(Tom *stands by the door beginning to think back— his raincoat in his hand, but still dragging on the floor.*)

Isn't there?—Of course there is. Who was it, or don't you want to tell?

Tom. May I have a cigarette?

Laura. *(Relieved that she has won another moment's delay.)* Yes. Of course. *(She hands him a box, then lights it for him.)*

Tom. My seventh grade teacher.

Laura. What?

Tom. That's who I remember.

Laura. Oh.

Tom. Miss Middleton—

Laura. How sweet.

Tom. *(Drops the raincoat again, and moves into the room.)* It wasn't sweet. It was terrible.

Laura. At that time, of course. Tell me about her.

Tom. She was just out of college—tall, blond—honey colored hair—and she wore a polo coat, and drove a convertible.

Laura. Sounds very fetching.

Tom. Ever since then I've been a sucker for girls in polo coats.

Laura. *(Smiling.)* I have one somewhere.

Tom. Yes, I know. *(He looks at her.)*

Laura. What happened?

Tom. What could happen? As usual I made a fool of myself. I guess everyone knew I was in love with her. People I like, I can't help showing it.

Laura. That's a good trait.

Tom. When she used to go on errands and she needed one of the boys to go along and help carry something— There I was.

LAURA. She liked you too, then.

TOM. This is a stupid thing to talk about.

LAURA. I can see why she liked you.

TOM. I thought she loved me. I was twelve years old.

LAURA. Maybe she did.

TOM. Anyway, when I was in eighth grade, she got married. And you know what they made me do? They gave a luncheon at school in her honor, and I had to be the toastmaster and wish her happiness and everything. I had to write a poem— *(He quotes.)*

"Now that you are going to be married,
> And away from us be carried,
> Before you promise to love, honor, and obey,
> There are a few things I want to say."

(He shakes his head as they BOTH *laugh.)*
From there on it turned out to be more of a love poem than anything else.

LAURA. *(As she stops laughing.)* Puppy love can be heart-breaking.

TOM. *(The smile dying quickly as he looks at her.)* I'm always falling in love with the wrong people.

LAURA. Who isn't?

TOM. You too?

LAURA. It wouldn't be any fun if we didn't. Of course, nothing ever comes of it, but there are bitter-sweet memories, and they can be pleasant. *(Kidding him as friend to friend—trying to get him to smile again.)* Who else have you been desperately in love with?

TOM. *(He doesn't answer. Then he looks at his watch.)* 's almost nine—I'm late. *(Starts to go.)*

LAURA. I can't persuade you to stay?

(TOM shakes his head, "no.")
e were getting on so well.

TOM. Thanks.

LAURA. In another moment I would have told you all the deep, dark secrets of my life.

TOM. I'm sorry. *(He picks up his coat from the floor.)*

LAURA. *(Desperately trying to think of something to keep him from going.)* Won't you stay even for a dance?

Tom. I don't dance.

Laura. I was going to teach you. *(She goes over to the phonograph and snaps on the button.)*

Tom. *(Opens the door.)* Some other time—

Laura. Please, for me. *(She comes back.)*

Tom. *(Closes the door.)* Tell me something.

Laura. Yes?

(The RECORD starts to play something soft and melodic.)

Tom. Why are you so nice to me?

Laura. Why— I—

Tom. You're not this way to the rest of the fellows.

Laura. No, I know I'm not. Do you mind my being nice to you?

Tom. *(Shakes his head, "no.")* I just wondered why.

Laura. *(In a perfectly open way.)* I guess, Tom— I guess it's because I like you.

Tom. No one else seems to. Why do you?

Laura. I don't know— I—

Tom. Is it *because* no one else likes me? Is it just pity?

Laura. No, Tom, no, of course not— It's, well—it's because you've been nice to me—very considerate. It wasn't easy for me, you know, coming into a school, my first year.—You seemed to sense that. I don't know, we just seem to have hit it off. *(She smiles at him.)*

Tom. Mr. Reynolds knows you like me.

Laura. I suppose so. I haven't kept it a secret.

Tom. Is that why he hates me so?

Laura. I don't think he hates you.

Tom. Yes, he hates me. Why lie? I think everyone here hates me but you. But they won't.

Laura. Of course they won't.

Tom. He hates me because he made a flop with me. I know all about it. My father put me in this house two years ago, and when he left me he said to your husband, "Make a man out of him." He's failed, and he's mad, and then you came along, and were nice to me—out of pity.

LAURA. No, Tom, not pity. I'm too selfish a woman to like you just out of pity.

TOM. *(He has worked himself up into a state of confusion, and anger, and desperation—)* There's so much I don't understand.

LAURA. *(Reaches out and touches his arm.)* Tom, don't go out tonight.

TOM. I've got to. That's one thing that's clear. I've got to!

LAURA. *(Holds up her arms for dancing.)* Won't you let me teach you how to dance?

TOM. *(Suddenly and impulsively he throws his arms around her, and kisses her passionately, awkwardly—and then in embarrassment he buries his head in her shoulder.)* Oh, God— God.

LAURA. Tom— Tom—

(TOM raises his face and looks at her, and would kiss her again.)

No, Tom— No, I—

(At the first "No," TOM breaks from her and runs out the door, halfway up the stairs.)

(Calling.) Tom! Tom!

(TOM stops at the sound of her voice and turns around and looks down the stairs.)

(LAURA moves to the open door.) Tom, I—

(The front door opens and one of the mountain-climbing boys—PHIL—comes in, with his pack.)

PHIL. *(Seeing TOM poised on the stairs.)* What the hell are you doing?

(TOM just looks at him.)

What's the matter with you? *(He goes on and up the stairs.)*

TOM. What are you doing back?

PHIL. The whole bunch is back. Who wants to go mountain climbing in the rain?

BILL. *(Outside his study door.)* Say, any of you fellows want to go across the street for something to eat when you get changed, go ahead.
           *(*PHIL *goes up the stairs past* TOM.*)*
*(*BILL *goes into his own room, leaving door open.)* Hi. *(He leaves off his equipment.)*

LAURA. *(Has been standing motionless where* TOM *has left her.)* Hello.

BILL. *(Comes to her and kisses her on the cheek.)* One lousy week-end a year we got to go climbing and it rains. *(Throws the rest of his stuff down.)* The fellows are damned disappointed.

LAURA. *(Hardly paying any attention to him.)* That's too bad.

BILL. *(Going up to alcove.)* I think they wanted me to invite them down for a feed. But I didn't want to. I thought we'd be alone. *(He looks across at her.)*

LAURA. *(She is listening for footsteps outside.)* Sure.

*(*BILL *goes out through alcove.* LAURA *stoops and picks up raincoat which* TOM *has dropped and hides it in the cabinet by the fireplace.)*

BILL. *(Appears in door momentarily wiping his hands with towel.)* Boy it really rained. *(He disappears again.)*
        *(*LAURA *sadly goes to the door and slowly and gently closes it. When she is finished, she leans against the door, listening—hoping against hope that* TOM *will go upstairs. When* TOM *sees the door close, he stands there for a moment, turns his coat collar up and goes down the hall and out.)*
(Offstage as TOM *starts to go down the hall.)* We never even made it to the timberline. The rain started to come down. Another hour or so and we would have got to the hut and spent the night, but the fellows wouldn't hear of it.
        (The DOOR slams. LAURA *turns away from the study door in despair.)*
(Still offstage.) What was that?

LAURA. Nothing— Nothing at all.

BILL. *(Enters and gets pipe from mantelpiece.)* Good to get out, though. Makes you feel alive. Think I'll go out again next Saturday, alone. Won't be bothered by the fellows wanting to turn back. *(He has settled down in the chair intended for* TOM.)

(The School BELLS start to ring Nine.)

(BILL *reaches out his hand for* LAURA. *Standing by the door, she looks at his outstretched hand, as the LIGHTS fade, and*

THE CURTAIN FALLS

END OF ACT TWO

ACT THREE

The time is the next afternoon.

As the Curtain rises, TOM *is in his room. His door is shut
and bolted. He is lying on his back on the bed,
staring up at the ceiling.*

RALPH. *(He is at the hall phone.)* Hello, Mary—
Ralph— Yeah, I just wanted you to know I'd be a little
delayed picking you up— Yeah—everyone was taking a
shower over here, and there's only one shower for eight
guys. No it's not the same place as last night— The tea-
dance is at the Inn— *(He suddenly looks very uncomfortable.)* Look, I'll tell you when I see you— Okay—
(Almost whispers it.) I love you—

 (STEVE, RALPH'S *side kick, comes running in from
 the outside. He's all dressed up and he's got something to tell.)*

Yeah, Mary.— Well, I can't say it over again. Didn't you
hear me the first time? *(Loud so she'll hear it.)* Hi, Steve.

STEVE. Come on, get off. I got something to tell you.

RALPH. Mary— Mary, I'll get there faster if I stop
talking now— Okay? Okay— See you a little after four.
(He hangs up.) What the hell's the matter with you?

STEVE. Have you seen Tom?

RALPH. No.

STEVE. You know what the hell he did last night?

RALPH. What?

STEVE. He went and saw Ellie.

RALPH. Who are you bulling?

STEVE. No, honest. Ellie told Jackson over at the kitchen. Everybody knows now.

RALPH. What did he want to go and do a thing like that
for?

73

STEVE. But wait a minute. You haven't heard the half of it.

RALPH. Listen, I gotta get dressed. *(Starts upstairs— stops.)*

STEVE. *(On their way up the stairs.)* The way Ellie tells it, he went there, all the hell dressed up like he was going to the dance, and— *(They disappear up the stairs.)*

(BILL *after a moment, comes in the hall, and goes quickly up the stairs. He goes right into* AL *and* TOM'S *sitting room without knocking, we then hear him try the handle of* TOM'S *bedroom door.* TOM *looks at the door defiantly and sullenly.)*

BILL. *(Knocks sharply.)* Tom! *(Rattles door some more.)* Tom, this is Mr. Reynolds. Let me in.

TOM. I don't want to see anyone.

BILL. You've got to see me. Come on. Open up! I've got to talk to the Dean at four, and I want to speak to you first.

TOM. There's nothing to say.

BILL. I can break the door down. Then your father would have to pay for a new door. Do you want that? Are you afraid to see me?

   (TOM *after a moment, goes to the door and pulls back the bolt.)*

(Comes in quickly.) Well.

   (TOM *goes back and sits on the bed. Doesn't look at* BILL.)

Now I've got to have the full story. All the details so that when I see the Dean—

TOM. —You've got the full story. What the hell do you want?

BILL. *(With malicious pleasure on his face.)* We don't seem to have the full story.

TOM. When the school cops brought me in last night they told you I was with Ellie Martin.

BILL. That's just it. It seems you weren't *with* her.

TOM. What do you mean?

BILL. You weren't *with* her. You couldn't be *with* her. Do you understand what I mean?

TOM. *(Trying to brave it out.)* Who says so?

BILL. She says so. And she ought to know.

(TOM *turns away.*)

She says that you couldn't and that you jumped up and grabbed a knife in her kitchen and tried to kill yourself —and she had to fight with you and that's what attracted the school cops.

TOM. What difference does it make?

BILL. *(Righteously.)* I just wanted the record to be straight. You'll undoubtedly be expelled, no matter what —but I wanted the record straight.

TOM. *(Turning on him.)* You couldn't have stood it, could you, if I'd proved you wrong?

BILL. Where do you get off talking like that to a master?

TOM. You'd made up your mind long ago, and it would have killed you if I'd proved you wrong.

BILL. Talking like that isn't going to help you any.

TOM. Nothing's going to help. I'm gonna be kicked out, and then you're gonna be happy.

BILL. I'm not going to be happy. I'm going to be very sorry—sorry for your father.

TOM. All right, now you know. Go on, spread the news. How can you wait?

BILL. I won't tell anyone—but the Dean, of course.

TOM. And my father—

BILL. Perhaps—

TOM. *(After a long pause.)* And Mrs. Reynolds.

BILL. *(Looks at* TOM.*)* Yes— I think she ought to know. *(He turns and leaves the room—goes through the sitting room and up the stairs, calling "*RALPH.*")*

(TOM *closes the door and locks it, goes and sits down in the chair.*)

LAURA. *(As* BILL *goes upstairs to* RALPH, *she comes into the master's study. She is wearing a wool suit. She goes to the cabinet and brings out* TOM'S *raincoat. She moves with it to the door.)*

(There is a KNOCK at the door.)

(She opens the door.) Oh, hello, Mr. Lee.

HERB. *(Coming in. He seems for some reason rather pleased.)* Hello, Laura.

LAURA. Bill isn't in just now, though I'm expecting him any moment.

HERB. My train was twenty minutes late. I was afraid I'd missed him. We have an appointment with the Dean in a few minutes.

LAURA. *(Is coolly polite.)* Oh, I see.

HERB. Have I done something to displease you, Laura? You seem a little— (HERB *shrugs and makes a gesture with his hands meaning cool.)*

LAURA I'm sorry. Forgive me. Won't you sit down?

HERB. I remember that you were displeased at my leaving Tom in school a week ago. Well, you see I was right in a sense. Though, perhaps being a lady you wouldn't understand.

LAURA. I'm not sure that I do.

HERB. Well, now look here. If I had taken Tom out of school after that scandal with Mr.—uh—what was his name—the uh—

LAURA. Mr. Harris.

HERB. Yes. If I'd taken Tom out then, he would have been marked for the rest of his life.

LAURA. You know that Tom will be expelled, of course.

HERB. Yes, but the circumstances are so much more normal.

LAURA. *(After looking at him a moment.)* I think, Mr. Lee, I'm not quite sure, but I think, in a sense, you're proud of Tom.

HERB. Well.

LAURA. Probably for the first time you're proud of him because the school police found him out of bounds with a—

HERB. I shouldn't have expected you to understand. Bill will see what I mean.

(BILL *starts down the stairs.*)

LAURA. He probably will.

(BILL *comes in.*)

HERB. Bill.
BILL. Oh, hello, Herb.
    (HERB *looks from* LAURA *to* BILL. *Notices the coldness between them.*)
I was just up seeing Tom.
    HERB. Yes. I intend to go up after we've seen the Dean. How is he?
    BILL. All right?
    HERB. (*Expansive.*) Sitting around telling the boys all about it.
    BILL. No, he's in his room alone. The others are going to the tea dance at the Inn. Laura—
    (*Sees* LAURA *is crossing to alcove.*)
Oh, Laura, I wish you'd stay.

(LAURA *takes one step back into the room.*)

HERB. I was telling your wife here, trying to make her understand the male point of view on this matter. I mean, how being kicked out for a thing like this, while not exactly desirable is still not so serious. It's sort of one of the calculated risks of being a man. (*He smiles at his way of putting it.*)
    BILL. (*Preparing to tell* HERB.) Herb?
    HERB. Yes, Bill. I mean, you agree with me on that, don't you?
    BILL. Yes, Herb, only the situation is not exactly as it was reported to you over the phone. It's true that Tom went to this girl Ellie's place, and it's true that he went for the usual purpose— However— However, it didn't work out that way.
    HERB. What do you mean?
    BILL. Nothing happened.

HERB. You mean she wouldn't have him?

BILL. I mean Tom— I don't know—he didn't go through with it. He couldn't. *(He looks at* LAURA.) It's true. The girl says so. And when it didn't work, he tried to kill himself with a knife in the kitchen, and she struggled with him, and that brought the school cops, and that's that.

(HERB *sits down in Left arm chair bewildered.*)
I'm sorry, Herb. Of course the fact that he was with Ellie at her place is enough to get him expelled.

HERB. Does everyone know this?

BILL. Well, Ellie talks. She's got no shame—and this is apparently something to talk about.

LAURA. *(To* HERB.) Do you still think it will make a good smoking-car story?

BILL. What do you mean?

HERB. Why did he do it? Before, maybe he could talk it down, but to go do a thing like this and leave no doubts.

LAURA. In whose mind?

BILL. Laura, please.

LAURA. *(Angry.)* You asked me to stay. *(Starts to the alcove.)*

BILL. *(Flaring back at her.)* Well, now you've heard. We won't keep you.

LAURA. *(Knowing, without asking.)* Why did you want me to hear?

BILL. *(Going to her at alcove.)* I wanted you to know the facts. That's all. The whole story.

(LAURA *stands in the alcove.*)

HERB. Bill, Bill! Maybe there's some way of getting to this girl so she wouldn't spread the story.

BILL. I'm afraid it's too late for that.

HERB. I don't know. Some things don't make any sense. What am I going to do now?

LAURA. *(Re-entering.)* Mr. Lee, please don't go on drawing the wrong conclusions!

HERB. I'm drawing no conclusions. This sort of thing

can happen to a normal boy. But it's what the others will
think— Added to the Harris business. And that's all that's
important.

LAURA. Isn't it important what Tom thinks?

BILL. Herb, we'd better be getting on over to the
Dean's—

HERB. *(Indicating upstairs.)* Is he in his room?

BILL. Yes.

HERB. Packing?

BILL. No.

HERB. I told him to come to you to talk things over. Did
he?

BILL. No.

HERB. What am I going to say to him now?

BILL. We're expected at four.

HERB. I know. But I've got to go up. Maybe I should
have left him with his mother. She might have known what
to do, what to say— *(He starts out.)* You want to come
along with me?

BILL. *(Moving to hall.)* All right.

LAURA. Bill, I'd like to talk with you.

BILL. I'll be back. *(Goes with HERB to the landing.)*

(LAURA *exits in alcove, taking off her jacket.)*

HERB. Maybe I ought to do this alone.

BILL. He's probably locked in his bedroom.

(HERB *goes inside the sitting room.* BILL *stays on landing.*
    TOM *as he hears his father knocking on the bedroom
    door, stiffens.* HERB *tries the door handle.)*

HERB. *(Off.)* Tom— Tom—it's—it's Dad.

(TOM *gets up, but just stands there.)*

Tom, are you asleep? *(After a few moments, he reappears
on the landing. He is deeply hurt that his son wouldn't
speak to him.)* I think he's asleep.

BILL. *(Making a move to go in and get* TOM.*)* He can't
be—

HERB. *(Stops.)*—Yes, I think he is. He was always a sound sleeper. We used to have to drag him out of bed when he was a kid.

BILL. But he should see you.

HERB. It'll be better later, anyhow. *(He starts down the stairs, troubled, puzzled.)*

BILL. *(Following.)* I'll go right with you, Herb. *(He goes out through the alcove.* HERB *stays in the study.)*

TOM. *(When his father is downstairs, he opens his bedroom door and faintly calls.)* Dad?

(HERB *looks up, thinking he's heard something, but then figures it must have been something else.* RALPH, STEVE *and* PHIL *come crashing down the stairs, dressed for the tea dance, ad libbing comments about the girls at the dance.* TOM *closes his door. When they have gone, he opens it again and calls "Dad" faintly. When there is no response, he closes the door, and goes and lies on the bed.)*

BILL. *(Re-entering.)* Laura, I'm going to the Dean's now with Herb. I'm playing squash with the Headmaster at five. So I'll see you at the dining room at 6:30.

LAURA. *(Entering after him.)* I wish you'd come back here after.

BILL. Laura. I can't.

LAURA. Bill, I wish you would.

BILL. *(Sees that there is some strange determination in* LAURA'*s face.)* Herb, I'll be with you in a minute.—Why don't you walk along

HERB. All right.—Goodbye, Laura. See you again.

BILL. You'll see her in a couple of days at the reunion.

HERB. I may not be coming up for it now— Maybe I will— I don't know. I'll be walking along. Goodbye, Laura. —Tell Tom I tried to see him. *(He goes out.)*

BILL. Now, Laura, what's the matter? I've got to get to the Dean's rooms to discuss this matter.

LAURA. Yes, of course. But first I'd like to discuss the

boys who made him do this—the men and boys who made him do this.

BILL. No one made him do anything.

LAURA. Is there to be no blame, no punishment for the boys and men who taunted him into doing this? What if if he had succeeded in killing himself? What then?

BILL. You're being entirely too emotional about this.

LAURA. If he had succeeded in killing himself in Ellie's rooms, wouldn't you have felt some guilt?

BILL. I?

LAURA. Yes, you.

BILL. I wish you'd look at the facts and not be so emotional about this.

LAURA. The facts! What facts! An innocent boy goes swimming with an instructor—an instructor whom he likes because this instructor is one of the few who encourage him, who don't ride him.—And because he's an off-horse, you and the rest of them are only too glad to put two and two together and get a false answer—anything which will let you go on and persecute a boy whom you basically don't like. If it had happened with Al or anybody else, you would have done nothing.

BILL. It would have been an entirely different matter. You can't escape from what you are—your character. Why do they spend so much time in the law courts on character witnesses? To prove this was the kind of man who could or could not commit such a crime.

LAURA. I resent this judgment by prejudice. He's not like me, therefore, he is capable of all possible crimes. He's not one of us—a member of the tribe!

BILL. *(Shows impatience—ready to leave.)* Now look, Laura, I know this is a shock to you, because you were fond of this boy. But you did all you could for him, more than anyone would expect. After all, your responsibility doesn't go beyond—

LAURA. —I know. Doesn't go beyond giving him tea and sympathy on Sunday afternoons. Well, I want to tell you something. It's going to shock you—but I'm going to tell you.

BILL. Laura, it's late.

LAURA. Last night I knew what Tom had in mind to do.

BILL. How did you know?

LAURA. I heard him making the date with Ellie on the phone.

BILL. And you didn't stop him? Then you're the one responsible.

LAURA. Yes, I am responsible, but not as you think. I did try to stop him, but not by locking him in his room, or calling the school police. I tried to stop him by being nice to him, by being affectionate. By showing him that he was liked—yes, even loved. I knew what he was going to do—and why he was going to do it. He had to prove to you bullies that he was a man, and he was going to prove it with Ellie Martin. Well— Well, last night—last night, I wished he had proved it with me.

BILL. What in Christ's name are you saying?

LAURA. Yes, I shock you. I shock myself. But you are right. I am responsible here. I know what I should have done. I knew it then. My heart cried out for this boy in his misery—a misery imposed by my husband. And I wanted to help him as one human being to another—and I failed. At the last moment, I sent him away—sent him to—

BILL. You mean you managed to overcome your exaggerated sense of pity.

LAURA. No, it was not just pity. My heart in its own loneliness— Yes, I've been lonely here, miserably lonely —and my heart in its loneliness cried out for this boy— cried out for the comfort he could give me too.

BILL. You don't know what you're saying.

LAURA. But I was a good woman. Good in what sense of the word? Good to whom—and for whom?

BILL. Laura, we'll discuss this, if we must, later on—

LAURA. Bill! There'll be no later on. I'm leaving you.

BILL. Over this thing?

LAURA. Yes, this *thing*, and all the other *things* in our marriage.

BILL. For God's sake, Laura, what are you talking about?

LAURA. I'm talking about love and honor and manliness, and tenderness, and persecution. I'm talking about a lot. You haven't understood any of it.

BILL. Laura, you can't leave over a thing like this. You know what it means.

LAURA. I wouldn't worry too much about it. When I'm gone, it will probably be agreed by all that I was an off-horse too, and didn't really belong to the clan, and it's good riddance.

BILL. And you're doing this—all because of this—this fairy?

LAURA. *(After a moment.)* This boy, Bill—this boy is more of a man than you are.

BILL. Sure— Ask Ellie.

LAURA. Because it was distasteful for him. Because for him there has to be love. He's more of a man than you are.

BILL. Yes, sure.

LAURA. Manliness is not all swagger and swearing and mountain climbing. Manliness is also tenderness, gentleness, consideration.—You men think you can decide on who is a man, when only a woman can really know.

BILL. Ellie's a woman. Ask Ellie.

LAURA. I don't need to ask anyone.

BILL. What do you know about a man? Married first to that boy—again, a poor pitiable boy.—You want to mother a boy, not love a man. That's why you never really loved me. Because I was not a boy you could mother.

LAURA. You're quite wrong about my not loving you. I did love you— But not just for your outward show of manliness, but because you needed me.—For one unguarded moment you let me know you needed me, and I have tried to find that moment again the year we've been married.—Why did you marry me, Bill? In God's name, why?

BILL. Because I loved you. Why else?

LAURA. —You've resented me—almost from the day you married me, you've resented me. You never wanted to marry really.—Did they kid you into it? Does a would-be headmaster have to be married? Or what was it, Bill?— You would have been far happier going off on your jaunts with the boys, having them to your rooms for feeds and bull-sessions—

BILL. That's part of being a master.

LAURA. Other masters and their wives do not take two boys with them whenever they go away on vacations or week-ends.

BILL. They are boys without privileges.

LAURA. And I became a wife without privileges.

BILL. You became a wife— *(He stops.)*

LAURA. Yes?

BILL. You did *not* become a wife.

LAURA. I know. I know I failed you. In some terrible way I've failed you.

BILL. You were more interested in mothering that fairy up there than in being my wife.

LAURA. But you wouldn't let me, Bill. You wouldn't let me.

BILL. *(Grabbing her by the shoulders.)* What do you mean I wouldn't let you?

LAURA. *(Quietly, almost afraid to say it.)* Did it ever occur to you that you persecute in Tom, that boy up there, you persecute in him the thing you fear in yourself?

(BILL looks at her for a long moment of hatred. She has hit close to the truth he has never let himself be conscious of. There is a moment when he might hurt her, but then he draws away, still staring at her. He backs away, slowly, and then turns to the door.)

Bill!

BILL. *(Not looking at her.)* I hope you will be gone when I come back from dinner.

LAURA. *(Quietly.)* I will be— *(Going towards him.)* Oh, Bill, I'm sorry. I shouldn't have said that—it was cruel. *(She reaches for him as he goes out the door.)* This was the weakness you cried out for me to save you from, wasn't it— And I have tried. *(He is gone.)* I have tried. *(Slowly she turns back into the room and looks at it.)* I did try.

(For a few moments she stands stunned and tired from her outburst. Then she moves slowly to Tom's *raincoat, picks it up and turns and goes out of the room and to the stair-landing. She goes to the sitting room door and knocks.)* Tom. *(She opens it and goes in, out of sight. At* Tom's *door, she calls again.)* Tom.

*(*Tom *turns his head slightly and listens.)*

*(*Laura *opens* Tom's *door and comes in.)* Oh, I'm sorry. May I come in? *(She sees she's not going to get an answer from him, so she goes in.)* I brought your raincoat. You left it last night. *(She puts it on chair. She looks at him.)* This is a nice room— I've never seen it before.—As a matter of fact I've never been up here in this part of the house. *(Still getting no response, she goes on.)*

> *(*Tom *slowly turns and looks at her back, while she is examining something on the walls.)*

(She turns, speaking.) It's very cozy. It's really quite—
> *(She stops when she sees he has turned around looking at her.)*

Hello.

Tom. *(Barely audible.)* Hello.

Laura. Do you mind my being here?

Tom. You're not suppose to be.

Laura. I know. But everyone's out, and will be for some time— I wanted to return your raincoat.

Tom. Thank you. *(After a pause, he sits up on the bed, his back to her.)* I didn't think you'd ever want to see me again.

Laura. Why not?

Tom. After last night. I'm sorry about what happened downstairs.

Laura. *(She looks at him a while, then:)* I'm not.

Tom. *(Looks at her. Can't quite make it out.)* You've heard everything, I suppose.

Laura. Yes.

Tom. Everything?

Laura. Everthing.

Tom. I knew your husband would be anxious to give you the details.

LAURA. He did. *(She stands there quietly looking down at the boy.)*

TOM. So now you know too.

LAURA. What?

TOM. That everything they said about me is true.

LAURA. Tom.

TOM. Well, it is, isn't it?

LAURA. Tom?

TOM. I'm no man. Ellie knows it. Everybody knows it. It seems everybody knew it, except me. And now I know it.

LAURA. *(Moves towards him.)* Tom— Tom—dear.

(TOM turns away from her.)

You don't think that just because—

TOM. What else am I to think?

LAURA. *(Very gently.)* Tom, that didn't work because you didn't believe in it—in such a test.

TOM. I touched her, and there was nothing.

LAURA. You aren't in love with Ellie.

TOM. That's not supposed to matter.

LAURA. But it does.

TOM. I wish they'd let me kill myself.

LAURA. Tom, look at me.

(TOM shakes his head.)

Tom, last night you kissed me.

TOM. Jesus!

LAURA. Why did you kiss me?

TOM. *(Turns. suddenly.)* And it made you sick, didn't it? *(Turns away from her again.)*

LAURA. How can you think such a thing?

TOM. You sent me away—you— Anyway, when you heard this morning it must have made you sick.

LAURA. *(Sits on edge of bed.)* Tom, I'm going to tell you something.

(TOM won't turn.)

Tom.

(He still won't turn.)

It was the nicest kiss I've ever had—from anybody.

(TOM slowly turns and looks at her.)

Tom, I came up to say goodbye.

(Tom *shakes his head, looking at her.*)
I'm going away— I'll probably never see you again. I'm
leaving Bill.
(Tom *knits his brows questioning.*)
For a lot of reasons—one of them, what he's done to you.
But before I left, I wanted you to know, for your own
comfort, you're more of a man now than he ever was or
will be.
(Tom *snorts.*)
And one day you'll meet a girl, and it will be right.
(Tom *turns away in disbelief.*)
Tom, believe me.
    Tom. I wish I could. But a person knows—knows inside.
Jesus, do you think after last night I'd ever—(*He stops.
After a moment, he smiles at her.*) But thanks— thanks
a lot. (*He closes his eyes.*)

(Laura *looks down at him a long time. Her face shows the
    compassion and tenderness she feels for this miser-
    able boy. After some time, she turns, and goes out
    the door—a moment later she appears in the outer
    door. She pauses for a moment, then reaches out and
    closes it and stays inside.*)

Tom, *when he hears the door close his eyes open. He sees
    she has left his bedroom. Then in complete misery,
    he lies down on the bed, like a wounded animal, his
    head at the foot of the bed.*

Laura *in a few moments appears in the bedroom doorway.
    She stands there, and then comes in, always looking at
    the slender boy on the bed. She closes the bedroom
    door.*

Tom *hears the sound and looks around. When he sees she
    has come back, he turns around slowly, wonderingly,
    and lies on his back, watching her.*

Laura *seeing a bolt on the door, slides it to. Then she*

stands looking at Tom, *her hand at her throat. With a
slight and delicate movement, she unbuttons the top
button of her blouse, and moves towards* Tom. *When
she gets alongside the bed, she reaches out her hand,
still keeping one hand at her blouse.* Tom *makes no
move. Just watches her.*

Laura *makes a little move with the outstretched hand—
asking for his hand.* Tom *slowly moves his hand to
hers.)*

Laura. *(Stands there holding his hand and smiling
gently at him. Then she sits and looks down at the boy,
and after a moment, barely audible—)* And now—
nothing?
    *(*Tom's *other hand comes up and with both his hands
he brings her hand to his lips.)*
Laura. *(Smiles tenderly at this gesture, and after a
moment—)* Years from now—when you talk about this
—and you will—be kind. *(Gently she brings the boy's
hands towards her opened blouse, as the LIGHTS slowly
dim out—and—)*

THE CURTAIN FALLS

THE END

TEA AND SYMPATHY

PROPERTIES

Act I

(on stage)

tobacco tin
cigarette box with matches
ash tray
pipe bowl with two pipes
3 letters (Tad Fellows,
    card, extra)
Martini shaker
glass with olive and water
sewing kit with needles, etc.
costume dress
blouse of costume
2 travel folders
ash tray (tea table)
ash tray (desk)
pencils, pen, papers
pads, books and desk
telephone
costume hat
wastebasket
photograph
frill of costume
necklace with ring
lipstick
toothpaste, brush, guitar

(off stage)

field glasses
books
towel

tray with:
    2 cups and saucers
    2 spoons
    sugar cup with tongs
plate of cookies
creamer
bottle of milk
teapot with tea
teapot whistle
school bag with books
phonograph

Act II, Scene 1

(on stage)

tobacco pouch on desk
change desk chair
extra crumpled paper on
    desk
tea table above chair
doors closed (except dbl.)
book of poems
crumpled wrapping paper
Tom's raincoat in closet
Dime for Jack
baseball
cigarette still on mantel

(off stage)

towel (Al's room)
tray with cookies and all
school bag with exams, etc.
book of poems wrapped

Scene 2

(on stage)

liquor cabinet door open 4"
curtains open
shade down in Tom's room
coffee cup with coffee
gumdrops and candy plate
doors closed except left dbl.
    door, and study door
    open 4"

(off stage)

towel

Act III
(on stage)

stool center and up
shade up in Tom's room
tea table struck
raincoat in bottom closet

(off left)

school bag

PROPERTY PLOT

ACT ONE

Bring in a pint of milk.
Also: 1 orange, 1 lemon, assorted cookies and soft candy.
    Cube ice in pitcher. Put on hot plate: water for tea.
Vacuum stage and set Act I furniture on marks. Make up
    bed in Tom's room and set two towels off back of
    bedroom.
Check binoculars off Left in bedroom. Also soft-ball.
Have tube of green toothpaste on Tom's bureau.
Get study ready:
    Skirt of costume on the stool.
    Sewing basket on the ottoman.
    Piece of material for sewing on floor near leg of chair
        Right.
    Cocktail glass with ice, water and olive on tea table.
    Framed picture on the desk.
    On Laura's chair: travel folders, and top of costume.
    ½ pint of whiskey in paper bag on bureau in Tom's
        room.
    Three letters on mantel of fireplace.
    Pipes and pipe tobacco on mantel of fireplace.

Off-stage Right:

    Tray with sugar bowl and two cups and saucers. Also, separate: cream pitcher and pint of milk. Tea-pot. Plate of assorted cookies. Glass of water with lemon and ice for Laura.

Off-stage up Center:

    Books for boys. Hiking clothes and props. School bag with books and exam papers for Bill.

ACT TWO—Scene I

Strike dress and sewing basket.

Put picture back on the desk.

Set furniture back on marks.

Make up bed.

Open window for rain effect (this means *curtains* of small window in study).

Put book and wrapping paper on arm chair stage Right.

Strike towel on stairway.

Have book of poems wrapped in store paper for Mr. Erick-son off up Center.

Off-stage Right: Tea tray complete with tea-pot, two cups and saucers, spoons, sugar and cream, and plate of cookies.

ACT TWO—Scene II

In fast change (forty seconds) do following:

    Pull down window shade in boy's room. Make up bed. Soft ball goes on radiator in boy's room.

    Strike tea set. Bring on cup of black coffee. Also plate of chocolates and gumdrops

    Strike pair of shoes and book and wrapping paper from arm chair.

    Close double door on off stage Right side only.

On opening of second scene get a pail of water ready to use in getting actors wet.

ACT THREE

Set back furniture on marks.

Fix up bed.
Strike coffee and candy.
Close curtains.
Fix raincoat and fold and put in bottom bin.
Strike the coffee table.
Off stage up Center:
  ½ orange for actor in opening of scene.
  Newspapers or comics.

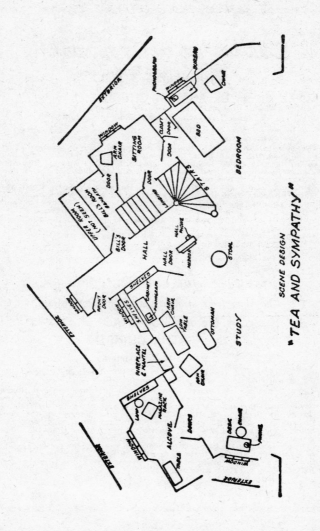

SCENE DESIGN

"TEA AND SYMPATHY"

Witness for the Prosecution

Melodrama—3 Acts

By AGATHA CHRISTIE

17 Men, 5 Women. Interior—Modern Costumes

*Winner of New York Critics Circle Award and the Antoinette
Perry Award. One of the greatest mystery melodramas in years.*

The story is that of a likable young drifter who is suspected of
bashing in the head of a middle-aged, wealthy spinster who has
willed her tidy estate to him. His only alibi is the word of his wife,
a queer customer, indeed, who, in the dock, repudiates the alibi and
charges him with the murder. Then a mystery woman appears with
damaging letters against the wife and the young man is freed. We
learn, however, that the mystery woman is actually the wife, who
has perjured herself because she felt direct testimony for her husband
woud not have freed him. But when the young man turns his back
on his wife for another woman, we realize he really was the murderer.
Then Miss Christie gives us a triple-flip ending that leaves the audience gasping, while serving up justice to the young man.

(ROYALTY, $50-$25.)

The Mousetrap

The longest-run straight play in London history.

Melodrama—3 Acts

By AGATHA CHRISTIE

5 Men, 3 Women—Interior

*The author of Ten Little Indians and Witness for the Prosecu-
tion comes forth with another English hit.*

About a group of strangers stranded in a boarding house during a
snow storm, one of whom is a murderer. The suspects include the
newly married couple who run the house, a spinster, an architect, a
retired Army major, a strange little man who claims his car over-
turned in a drift, and a feminine jurist. Into their midst comes a
policeman, traveling on skiis. He no sooner arrives than the jurist
is killed. To get to the rationale of the murderer's pattern, the policeman probes the background of everyone present, and rattles a lot
of skeletons. Another famous Agatha Christie switch finish! Chalk
up another superb intrigue for the foremost mystery writer of her
half century. Posters and publicity.

(ROYALTY, $50-$25.)